Trust

Trust

A Radical Manifesto

Steve Chalke and Anthony Watkis

Authentic

10 09 08 07 06 05 04   7 6 5 4 3 2 1

First published in 2004 by Authentic Media
9 Holdom Avenue, Bletchley, Milton Keynes, MK1 1QR, UK
and
P.O. Box 1047, Waynesboro, GA 30830-2047, USA
Website: www.authenticmedia.co.uk

British Library Cataloguing in Publication Data
A catalogue record for this book is available from the British Library

ISBN 1-85078-586-4

Cover Design by Phil Houghton
Typeset by WestKey Ltd, Falmouth, Cornwall
Print Management by Adare Carwin
Printed and Bound in Denmark by AIT Norhaven AS

Contents

Acknowledgements

This book could not have been written without the help of a great many people. Special thanks must go to Joy Madeiros whose clarity of thought and depth of knowledge has shaped so many of these pages; to Jeff Russell and the team at Faithworks Poole whose work has inspired so many and now, through this book, whose story will do the same; to Christine Foster, without whom this book would still be a collection of thoughts on scraps of paper scattered across our desks; to Nathan Oley who came back just in time; and to the rest of the Faithworks team, who were a patient sounding board for ideas and an inexhaustible source of material.

Though their material contribution to this work was limited, our heartfelt thanks go to the following people who offered us endless love, support and encouragement as we burnt the midnight oil to write it: Cornelia Chalke; Chloe Stirling-Smith; Simon Johnston; Pete Brierley; Ted and Barbara Watkis; Jo Coles and Phil Hoyle; Judith Doel; Ro Leech; Al Briggs; Ryan, Luke, Wayne, Rachel and the rest of the guys at the Church.co.uk Centre.

Foreword

Trust is a very basic commodity in any social interaction. When trust goes missing we are doomed to dysfunction – and it has been sought and found absent in so many areas of our society of late. The casualties of this breakdown are many and various. Privately and publicly, as trust has been worn away, relationships of every kind have suffered. And society is nothing save for a complex web of relationships; or as the German theologian, Jurgen Moltmann reminds us, public life is a *'densely woven fabric of promises and promise keeping'* which cannot exist without trust.

Politicians have seldom been trusted less than now. Of the 650 Members of Parliament, the vast majority are hard working and professional people committed to the common good. But in any opinion poll you care to mention, political leadership is trailing badly in the trust awards. The easy option is to conclude that we get the politicians we deserve. But in a liberal democracy, I suspect it's even more likely that we get the politicians we *create*.

A wider perspective reveals that it isn't solely politicians who are no longer imbued with trust – scarcely an institution, industry, or individual has failed to notice the effects of the decline of trust in their relationships.

This has far-reaching ramifications for the Church – whose very existence is relational. Where trust fails, so relationships fail; and where relationships crumble, so the Church collapses.

This timely, thought provoking and debate-inducing book from Faithworks does not bemoan society's ills, but rather provides an agenda for private citizens and public servants to work in a critical partnership to rebuild society by recovering trust. We each have a part to play. I commend it to you as a tool for change.

Joel Edwards
General Director, Evangelical Alliance

One

A Radical Manifesto

'Our distrust is very expensive.'
Ralph Waldo Emerson

Trust – it's a little word but a big concept. Trust was once in abundant supply; generously given and freely received. Politicians, policemen, doctors, journalists and vicars; all were seen as pillars of the community who could and should, by virtue of their office, rely on being invested with great trust and respect.

Today things are different. The government, the media, the royal family, the church, the police, the law lords and many more have tumbled from their pedestals. Politicians, we reckon, are probably lying to us – covering up the truth in order to serve their own ends. Policemen are likely to be corrupt, brutal racists. Journalists are hooked on sales and sensation rather than truth and integrity. And vicars! Vicars are either rather wet simpletons who don't even really believe the message they earn a living from, or sexual deviants preying on the more vulnerable members of their flock.

It is small wonder, therefore, that trust, or the lack of it, is now the focus of countless column inches, news reports, chat shows and documentaries, not to mention pub conversations. The problem is that much of what is said is nothing more than a pointless commentary on the fact of trust's disappearance; bemoaning the situation we find ourselves in and expressing a yearning for things to be different – a kind of 'If only we could turn the clock back' mentality. However, as a wise man once explained, 'Stupidity is doing tomorrow what you did yesterday and expecting a different result.' Trust won't just reappear out of thin air – we need to adopt a more constructive approach to our problem.

'I think we may safely trust a good deal more than we do.'
Henry David Thoreau

We would all like to live in a world filled with trust, but we don't. The important question, therefore, is what are we going to do about it? We have a stark choice. Trust won't just happen because we want it to. Therefore, we can either keep behaving as we are now and get used to the way things are, or take some action designed to reverse our plight. And if action is going to be taken, then it's high time to take the first steps.

For the Church, at least, much of this journey is about what it means to live out our faith in the new context in which we find ourselves at the start of the twenty-first century – a minority group in a postmodern, post-Christendom culture. The challenge of this is to learn to live (as many Old Testament biblical characters, such as Daniel in Babylon, had to do) with the shift from a culture where we had power, to one in which we need to work hard to find influence.

In the end, to say that our society no longer trusts its big institutions is simply another way of recognising that it has lost faith in them. The Church can no longer demand that society automatically believes it to be faith-worthy.

Instead it must learn how to work hard to win favour as it demonstrates a faith that works.

Hard Talk

Building trust is a difficult and time-consuming business that requires a lot of hard and sustained work. Trust can be encouraged or eroded by our behaviour. It evolves over time and with experience. It can't be rushed or hurried. It has to be earned. But, as expensive as it is to develop, trust is vital to every aspect of life; not just publicly but privately, not just collectively but individually. The task of this book is, therefore, to analyse the key components on which trust is built and so consider the processes by which it is either developed or destroyed. It will explore the benefits of being trusted. It will examine practical ways in which trust can be built. It will then specifically ask hard questions of both government and Church as they both strive to become more trusted by the public and each other.

There are countless commentaries, some very good, some superficial, on the reasons for the erosion of trust in society today. The primary aim of this book is not to add to them. Rather than a catalogue of reasons for failure, this book is a manual for reconstruction. Any analysis of the past that we engage in is to enable us in our real task – to answer the all-important question of where should we be heading now. In a world where trust has been eroded, is it possible to become agents of change – building trust instead of laying blame?

The title of this book is *Trust – A Radical Manifesto*. What is our radical manifesto concerning trust? It is simply this. Rather than spending our time worrying about and bemoaning its loss, we commit ourselves, as individuals and institutions, to become those who demonstrate a new trustworthiness. For the challenge of the moment set before us all – from government to Church, media to business leaders and ordinary individuals to royal family – is simply this: consistently to adopt behaviours that rebuild trust. Or, if we will not, to watch as our society slowly disintegrates.

Though the title of this book is *Trust* (in fact, *because* the title of this book is *Trust)*, its content is more accurately about something else, something closely related, but something subtly different – trustworthiness. The reason is simple. The key question we all face is not so much 'Why don't people trust me?' as 'What can I do to become worthy of their trust?'

Ebb and Flow

In generations past a person was to be trusted unless they proved themselves to be unworthy of it – trust was society's default setting. Today, however, most people want to be safe rather than sorry. Trust is no longer automatic. The new rule is 'guilty until proven innocent'. Trust has to be earned the hard way.

> *'Who would rather not trust and be deceived?'*
> Eliza Cook, 19th century poet.

Trust is never a simple 'on' or 'off' affair. Though once established it can survive great disappointments, when it is abused, even where it has been developed over years, it will be damaged. Trust is like money in the bank. While one withdrawal will not necessarily take you into the red, if over time funds only flow out, eventually even the richest account will be emptied. However, the reverse is also true: the more deposits we make (however small), the more credit we collect. The building or breakdown of trust, then, is normally incremental. Though, in some cases, an act of betrayal is enough to destroy it immediately, most of the time its ebb and flow are gradual. Which means that, for trust to have become such a scarce commodity in our society, we must perceive ourselves to have been disappointed and let down very often.

Brave New World

There are many reasons why, for instance, trust in the government and politicians in general has diminished over the years. No doubt the behaviour of specific individuals and groups of politicians who have not lived up to the trust bestowed upon them has significantly impacted the situation. The actions of characters such as Lord Jeffrey Archer, Dame Shirley 'homes for votes' Porter and the scandal surrounding Dr David Kelly's death and the search for 'Weapons of Mass Destruction' have done little to convince the public to trust our political leaders. However, it is simplistic in the extreme to conclude that the breakdown of trust in politics is entirely the fault of individual politicians. There is no objective means of comparison between those in office today and their counterparts of, say, one hundred years ago, but it would not be unreasonable to assert that the behaviour of our current crop of politicians is no worse than that of generations past. In fact, it is generally far better and they are required to be far more accountable.

Our society is different for all sorts of reasons to the way it was a century ago. We don't want to turn the clock back. We can't turn the clock back – and even if we could it would only read the wrong time! Instead we want to, need to, face the challenges of life in the early twenty-first century; the world of 24/7 media coverage, message management and information overload. And we have to face a new world which poses new challenges for us, requires new skills of us, but also creates new opportunities for us.

> *'Trust is the watchword for everyone here at the BBC –*
> *we're independent, impartial and honest.'*
>
>   BBC Values Statement

Some have argued that the greatest single reason for the absence of trust in society is the role of the media. Nothing in life today is hidden from its glare. Nothing is private, nothing secure, nothing sacred; everything is vulnerable to being leaked, uncovered or 'outed'. In the past someone had to mess up extremely badly before the public found out. Today, however, there is rarely a single week without an exposé of some sort breaking. But though bad news sells papers, the impact of repeated reports of a lack of personal or corporate integrity naturally tarnishes our understanding of people and institutions generally. And each news report telling tales of sleaze, negligence or mismanagement represents another withdrawal from the bank account of trust. Or to put it another way, no single wave will destroy a coastline: however, the repeated crash of thousands of small waves will eventually cause even giant cliffs to crumble into the sea.

> *'Journalists who used to dine with politicians now dine*
> *on them.'*
>
>   Geoff Mulgan

But if the media has been partly responsible for the decline of trust in society, it has also fallen victim of its own sword. The public no longer considers that the words it reads and the reports it hears carry the weight they once did. For instance, Andrew Gilligan's report of the 'sexed up' 45 minute claim in the government's Iraq Dossier, and the subsequent scandal that emerged, did significant damage to public perception of the media's trustworthiness as well as the government's. A recent MORI poll reported that while 92% of people trust doctors, a mere 20% trust journalists. How can we believe what we are told if there is the suspicion that the writers are inventing or 'sexing up' the stories themselves?

Pointing the Finger

Before pointing the finger at someone else, it is important to remember that when you do, three more point straight back at you. Like it or not, the Church in the UK is hardly in a position to preach any sermons on trust to its surrounding culture. There have been endless tales of the abuse of power by leaders of all denominations. It is a tragic fact that, in the perception of many, Roman Catholic priests are identified with paedophilia and Anglican vicars with repressed homosexuality. But the ministers of the lesser denominations are also viewed with deep suspicion – to the average man on the street, a charismatic or community church and a cult are not far apart.

There is, however, a greater reason why trust in the Church has declined. Over the years the Church's role in society has changed radically. In centuries past we played an important role at the hub of the community. The Church was the sole provider of medical care, education and just about every form of social welfare available. That is no longer the case. Where once our reason for existing was to serve the community and, in so doing, demonstrate God's love and our trustworthiness, the Church has nowadays become principally known for Sunday morning services. We cannot hope to be trusted if our message is not consistent with our actions.

> *'There's clearly quite a lot to that little word trust. And the more you examine it, the more important it becomes to our overall sense of security – the sense that we are standing on solid ground.'*
>
> Rowan Williams

When Trust Fails

We have looked at some of the ways in which trust has been eroded, but how does its loss affect society?

The cost society carries as a result of the breakdown of trust is extremely high. When we stop trusting we withdraw, we stop participating, we cease to engage. If you don't trust in the Church, you are more than likely to stop being part of it. If you don't believe the reports in newspapers, you are increasingly likely to stop reading them. And if you don't have faith in politicians, you are less likely to vote.

So it was that the 2001 general election yielded the second lowest turnout of voters in the history of modern British democracy (just over 59%, the lowest since 1918). This is alarming for the health of political democracy. It reveals one of two things; either that a huge number of those eligible to vote don't care who is elected to govern them or that, in a world of spin and counter-spin which is all about show rather than substance – a world in which we are all being manipulated anyway – it doesn't really matter who is pulling the strings. Either way, an enormous number of people have lost trust in the political process.

'You can't help but think that the sound bite and a scrap for the benefit of Jeremy Paxman don't really do justice to the democratic process.'

Tony Benn

In the run-up to the 2002 local elections there were adverts posted all over Croydon (the Greater London borough in which I live) asking the question 'What takes just two minutes but lasts four years?' The answer below simply said 'Your vote!' If that is the way in which democracy is advertised, then it is small wonder so few people can be bothered to participate. After all, non-involvement is a vote – a vote of no confidence! If the sum total of our involvement in the political process amounts to putting a cross on a form, surely we are all missing the point of democracy.

Democracy, as the saying goes, is the government of the people by the people. True democracy requires our active involvement; it brings responsibilities as well as privileges. However, by and large, we've left the world of politics to the professionals and sidelined ourselves. But in doing this we have subverted democracy – we have become uninvolved and uninterested and, as a result, society has paid the price.

'Man's capacity for justice makes democracy possible, but man's inclination to injustice makes democracy necessary.'

Reinhold Niebuhr

Rather than simply blaming others, it is time to acknowledge that central to our problems has been our political acquiescence. We need a new politics of community involvement and engagement. We cannot afford to leave the future of our society to the elite few any longer. Mature democracy demands our active involvement. But what came first, the chicken or the egg? Was it that in stepping back and letting the professionals handle government we lost touch and so lost trust in the system? Or was it that in losing trust we eventually stepped back and lost touch? Perhaps it's a vicious circle.

'I'm not really interested in politics.' Though commonly felt, this is a ridiculous sentiment. Politics is simply about the affairs of the people. It therefore concerns us all because it directly affects all of our lives – we are all on the receiving end of the policy decisions of both Whitehall and the town hall. Some people, of course, still champion our right to vote as if that, in and of itself, gives us democracy. They say that our forefathers fought for it. But what our forefathers and the suffragettes actually fought for was the right to be involved; to have a voice, not just a vote. It's easy to confuse the two, but when a voice is reduced to a vote, you soon lose the will to vote at all.

'We all get the government we deserve.'

Anonymous

The story is told of a government representative who paid a visit to a local farm. The farmer was out in the fields while his wife was working in the house but keeping a close eye on their eight-year-old daughter who was playing in the farmyard. The government visitor asked the girl if her mum and dad were around – but as he was doing this, her mother happened to look out of the open kitchen window and saw her young daughter talking to a stranger. Horrified, she called out at the top of her voice, 'Who are you talking to? Get in here with me, right now!' 'It's OK mummy' came the unconcerned response, 'he says he's from the government.' 'Well, in that case, get in here and bring the cow with you!'

The problem for us all is that the dominant mindset of our culture leads us to believe that there is always an instant, quick-fix, low cost, easy solution to any and every problem. But we are wrong; there isn't. Whether for the government, the Church, the media or big business, breaking the cycle of distrust and rebuilding trust in public life is going to be a long road which will require a deep and ongoing commitment to travel. In the next chapter we turn our attention to exploring how.

Two

Building Trust

*'One must be fond of people and trust them if one is not
to make a mess of life.'*

E.M. Forster

If the sense of trust in society has broken down over the
years, the question is, what practical steps can we take to
rebuild it? This chapter explores that issue. First, however,
let's look at the rewards of being invested with a greater
level of trust.

For government, achieving a greater sense of trust will
reduce the extent to which they are viewed with suspicion; rumours and scandals will carry less weight and the
electorate will be less apathetic and more engaged politi-
cally. For businesses, increased trust will keep customers,
partners and staff loyal; ultimately a trustworthy business
is a profitable business. For the Church, when and where
she is trusted, the public, the government and funders will
be more receptive both to the idea of working with her and
therefore, of course, far more open to her message. And for
individuals, where we are trusted our relationships will
be easier, deeper and more open; people will be more
likely to think the best of us, forgive us when we get it
wrong and consider our needs more readily.

The advantages of being trustworthy, then, are clear. The more that people trust us, the more they will:

- Actively seek our advice.
- Be inclined to accept and act on our recommendations.
- Treat us as we would wish to be treated.
- Respect us.
- Give us the benefit of the doubt.
- Forgive us when we make mistakes.
- Protect us when we need it.
- Warn us of dangers that we might avoid.
- Feel comfortable in their relationship with us.
- Allow us to feel comfortable with them.
- Work to decrease the level of bureaucracy involved in our interactions with them.
- Fund our work.

> *'Trust each other again and again. When the trust level gets high enough, people transcend apparent limits, discovering new and awesome abilities of which they were previously unaware.'*
>
> David Armistead

The First Step

The big question, then, is how do we go about generating trust? Unfortunately it isn't as simple as saying 'Trust me'. In fact, if trust isn't already there, calling for it becomes counter-productive. As we have already seen, if we want to enjoy the advantages of being trusted we must first work hard to demonstrate our trustworthiness. The classic Disney film *The Jungle Book* contains a scene in which Kaa, the oily boa constrictor, attempts to lure the 'man-cub' Mowgli into his lair – his malign intent is clear;

Mowgli would make a nice meal. Kaa fixes Mowgli with a hypnotic stare and sings to him 'Trust in me'. However, such trust would be misplaced. If we want to be trusted we need to do more than ask for it. We need to find ways of demonstrating that we will not abuse the trust we are given – of demonstrating that we are trustworthy.

In a recent survey pairs of people (students and teachers, husbands and wives, bosses and employees etc.) were individually asked which of them, in their relationship, had acted in the most trustworthy way. Perhaps unsurprisingly, everyone interviewed stated that they believed themselves to be the most trustworthy party. But more interestingly they also universally felt that the other person in the relationship, when asked, would have to agree with their assessment. Of course, none of them did! The first step towards becoming more trustworthy, then, is accepting that we might not be as trusted as we believe or would like. Certainly the Church is misguided in her belief that she is perceived as being trustworthy. Our society views the Church with the same suspicion that Mowgli should have had for the snake trying to ensnare him for his own gain – the collection plate is very hungry!

The Trust Equation

In order to become trustworthy in any relationship, it is vital to understand the essential characteristics of trust:

- Trust grows, rather than just appearing. It takes time, effort, will and work to gain trust – there is simply no short cut to building it. It develops slowly, evolving in any relationship over time.
- Trust is emotional as well as rational. Trust is not only a matter of cold intellectual understanding; it is just as

much an emotional feeling or response to someone and
their ideas.
- Trust is always dependent on a two-way relationship.
- Trust always involves taking risks.
- Trust is about personal perception and, therefore, it is
not always reciprocal. It is different for the individual
parties in a relationship. For instance, it is quite possible
that though you may trust someone implicitly, they
remain wary of you.

So what steps can we take to ensure that we are constantly
helping people to develop their trust in us? David Maister,
Rob Galford and Charles Green developed a 'trust equation' for business consultants that they use in a book called
The Trusted Advisor.[1] However, the concepts they talk of
have application far beyond the professional world of
consultancy that they are addressing. The basic principles
they use apply to the development and maintenance of
trust in all types of relationships – from marriage to neigh-
bours and work colleagues to wider family. We have,
therefore, adapted and rewritten their original trust
equation as:

$$T = \frac{C + D + R}{S}$$

$$\text{Trust} = \frac{\text{Credibility} + \text{Dependability} + \text{Relationship}}{\text{Self Interest}}$$

The next section of this chapter explores the importance
of these individual elements of trust. As we do so, we
will illustrate each of them from one of Faithworks local
networks (see p. 19) based in Poole, Dorset. Faithworks
Poole was the first of the now fast-growing number of

---

[1] David Maister, Rob Galford and Charles Green, *The Trusted Advisor* (Free Press, 2002).

town-wide groups of churches working together as part of the Faithworks movement.

Credibility

We will only be trusted when we are seen as being credible. People and partners with whom we deal must believe that we know what we are talking about and have the expertise to deliver tangible results.

Doctors and dentists often display their qualification certificates on their walls – not because they are bragging about their educational achievements, but rather to put their patients (people like us!) at ease. It's amazing how comforting it is to see a university certificate hanging on a wall, silently attesting to the fact that the person treating you has experience and expertise – it boosts your confidence as they plunge their needle in your arm or mouth!

Of course, there are other aspects of any healthcare surgery that also help to put us at ease. For instance, we know that when we visit the dentist they will almost certainly be wearing a white tunic and will take us into a brightly lit, clean and tidy, highly clinical room, containing a huge space-age chair. It is this combination of the certificates on the wall, the manner in which they present themselves, the familiar surroundings and usually the positive testimony of our friends and family that makes a medical practitioner credible. One would hardly feel comfortable consulting a dentist who, though highly qualified, experienced and technically proficient, worked in a dirty room with sawdust on the floor, wore a blood-stained butcher's apron and refused to make eye contact with their patients. Credibility is, then, both about expertise (what we can do) and presence (the way in which we do it).

Credibility has huge implications for the level of trust we invest into any relationship. If, for example, you can't drive and a friend offers to take you out for some lessons, you will only be able to trust them if they themselves are a qualified and competent driver. We only trust people if we perceive that they have the appropriate knowledge and expertise.

Credibility is a big issue for the Church, and for every local church and Christian project. In a recent survey people responded well to Jesus, believing him to be at very least a wise, open and relevant man. However, the same people, when asked about the Church, gave largely negative feedback – in their perception the Church is controlling, irrelevant and boring.

Furthermore, it isn't only the public that the Church has failed to convince. There can be little doubt that, though not always recognised as such, the Church is the largest single voluntary provider of social care in the UK. Consider the number of youth programmes, homeless shelters, pregnancy crisis centres, parents and toddlers groups, elderly people's lunch clubs, debt management services and the like that are operated by churches up and down the land. Each and every day the Church mobilises an army of volunteers and paid staff committed to caring for others, delivering annually millions of man-hours in free social welfare provision. And yet it often remains difficult for churches and Christian charities to attract partnership or funding from government and other secular bodies. Why? It's clear. They simply don't trust us as much as we would like.

A significant reason for this breakdown of trust is the issue of credibility or the lack of it. Local churches are either failing to demonstrate that they have sufficient expertise to manage community development and deliver quality projects successfully, or they do, in fact, lack that professional ability.

Credibility – A Faithworks Case Study

Faithworks Poole is a registered company with an explicit Christian ethos statement, seeking to provide opportunities for Christians to demonstrate their faith through projects created in partnership with the Borough of Poole Council. Officially launched in January 2004 with the full support of local politicians, it represents twenty-nine local churches working together and is presently developing projects working with children, rough sleepers, isolated older people and carers. (For more information on how to set up a local Faithworks network in your area see p. 89.) Faithworks Poole's core funding is provided by the local council and the borough's Local Strategic Partnership (LSP). Mandatory in every council, LSPs are the vehicle through which local authorities both listen to the views of the community and engage with other local organisations to make life better in their area. Typically an LSP (many of which go by friendlier names such as 'The Poole Partnership') contains representatives from local business, public services (the health service, education, the emergency services etc.), the voluntary sector (charities, churches and other faith groups) and the local council. Together their task is to find ways they can work in a joined up way to enhance the quality of life and breadth of services offered to the local community (for more on LSPs see p. 80).

Faithworks Poole has, within a short space of time, developed several partnerships with the local council, largely because both the chairperson and manager of Faithworks Poole have the credibility needed to build these relationships. The chair of Faithworks Poole has held the position of civic chaplain for some years (and as such is known and trusted by many of the local council) while the manager holds a position of principal officer in the local social services. So, though Faithworks Poole was not able to offer to the council a track record in delivering services, it did have individuals who had already proved themselves to be credible officers of the council through their paid functions. Both were, therefore, well known as people who understood and were able to work with local government cultures and systems.

Because of this credibility, the Local Strategic Partnership trusted Faithworks Poole to establish a faith communities website in order to provide a single access point for them to liaise with the faith communities of Poole. As an organisation, Faithworks Poole did not have any particular IT expertise and nor indeed were the chair or manager of Faithworks Poole known as individuals with any special IT or website skills. The funding was approved, however, because more generally the individuals, and therefore the entire entity, were regarded as being credible.

What practical steps can you take to increase your credibility? Here are some key principles:

1   Invest in getting the right training, experience and qualifications.
2   Get involved – find ways of serving, however small. Remember trust always evolves over time.
3   Use the contacts you make constantly to explore new ways of partnership and service.
4   Be honest all of the time. Never lie. Don't exaggerate what you can offer – if you 'talk-up' your abilities, though you might be trusted once, you won't be given a second chance.
5   If you don't know the answer to a question, say so quickly and directly – never be tempted to bluff to save face.

6   When you make a mistake, apologise and don't cover it up.

7   Sign the Faithworks Charter (discussed at length in the next chapter) the benchmark for professionalism for churches and charities in delivering community services – and then systematically work towards fulfilling it.

8   Love God and love people – when you do it *will* show and it *will* make a huge difference.

Dependability

Dependability is all about whether or not people perceive us as being reliable and consistent. It is about developing reputation. At its most simple, dependability is about delivering on what we promise to do, when we say we'll do it. For example, if you promise to phone someone at a certain time, you are only dependable if you do in fact call them at that time. And because other people's judgements on our dependability are slowly built up over time – the more interactions we have with someone – the clearer an idea they'll have about how dependable we are. In the end, dependability is a matter of track record.

Essentially we will only be perceived as being dependable if our actions are consistent with our words – and it's all too easy to get it wrong. We all know how amazingly easy it is to let people down. We frequently say things such as 'I'll call you later in the week', 'I'll be home at 7.30' or 'Can I borrow that book? I'll give it straight back', only to find that the pressures and busyness of life get in the way. These are only small things, but it is the small things of life that most greatly affect to what extent others view us as being dependable. We are measured on the length of time it takes us to reply to a voice mail message, or an e-mail, or our punctuality when it comes to ringing back, making meetings, remembering an anniversary, answering letters, passing on contracts or hitting deadlines.

However, when we deliver on the small things, slowly we find that we are trusted with more and more – it's a law of the universe. It's important, then, that we don't make promises that we can't deliver. We need to be sure that we don't overstate our abilities; our motto should always be 'under-promise and over-deliver.'

Dependability – A Faithworks Case Study

One of the first projects of Faithworks Poole is the five-year appointment of a worker whose task is to look at the spiritual needs of children in the care of Poole council – primarily children with foster parents. In this initiative, though the council has not provided direct funding (that comes from the Wessex region of the United Reformed Church) it has been very keen to work in partnership with Faithworks Poole to set up, support and resource this ground-breaking, even unique, project. Such has been the support from the council, that the Faithworks Poole project worker is located in the children and families section of social services, is regarded as a member of the fostering team and has all the office, IT and administrative support of a full council employee.

This partnership is a consequence of a long discussion between Faithworks Poole and the local social services, based around a shared commitment to the same high standards with regard to recruitment and selection and confidentiality (see chapter on the Faithworks Charter p. 47). Importantly, the Faithworks chairperson was committed to working to deliver appropriate funding. This was secured and thus a sense of Faithworks Poole's dependability was established. Partnerships with a local authority are not simply about the council always putting up the money. Here, Faithworks Poole itself had to be relied upon to come up

> with the direct salary costs, while the social services depart-
> ment had to demonstrate a willingness to break new ground
> and offer ongoing forms of support and indirect funding
> (office space, admin support etc.).

How can you build your sense of dependability? The following steps will help:

1   Make specific commitments to people around the
    small things: e.g. phoning back by the end of the day,
    e-mailing an address for tomorrow morning, send-
    ing the draft by Monday. And then deliver on them,
    quietly, and on time.
2   If you struggle to remember to do things, do them as
    they arise. For instance, whenever possible reply to
    an e-mail as soon as you open it.
3   Make sure meetings have clear outcomes, check
    what they are and then make sure that you meet
    them.
4   Consider how the person you are dealing with pre-
    fers things done and how they like to be treated.
5   Reconfirm scheduled events before they happen –
    and announce any changes to planned events as soon
    as they are changed.
6   Be honest about what you can do, as well as what you
    can't.
7   When you make a mistake or fail to meet a deadline –
    apologise.

Relationship

The most vital factor in building trust is relationship – and
ironically it is probably the most overlooked. Relationship

is essential to trust. What parent, for instance, would ever consider leaving their young child with a babysitter whom they didn't know?

Working relationships are no different to the relationships we build in our personal lives with our friends, husbands/wives or boyfriends/girlfriends. In order to build and maintain a healthy relationship, we have to work at being consistently and intentionally understanding, thoughtful, considerate, sensitive and supportive. Most importantly, forming strong and intimate bonds involves giving time and being around. It is exactly the same for our working relationships. It is remarkably easy, however, to overlook the need for these qualities in this context – we end up far too focused on simply getting the job done. They say 'It's not what you know, it's who you know', but the truth is that it has to be a bit of both. Trust grows where credibility, dependability and healthy relationships are present. If we invest time and energy into the people with whom we interact it is highly likely that, just as in our home lives, things will slowly begin to run more smoothly, disagreements will be less frequent, accomplishing tasks will become more enjoyable and trust will flourish. But more than this, and again just as in private life, integrity calls us to ensure that building and deepening relationships is not just a means to an end, but rather an end in itself. When it's not, our lack of integrity will soon be spotted.

Healthy relationships always require a level of vulnerability, openness and transparency, especially as they first start to develop. Though there is a risk of rejection involved in taking the first step in building a strong relationship, the only way to ensure that any relationship has a chance of growing is to initiate it yourself. Building trust always involves taking risks. In order to develop strong relationships we must take the risk of trusting other people. If we want our relationships to grow we have to be generous – we have to give a favour to earn a favour – there's no other way. By giving to a relationship as much or more than we take from it, we slowly prove ourselves to be trustworthy. And when we do make mistakes, in these strong relationships we will find that we will be much more easily forgiven.

Relationship – A Faithworks Case Study

Since 1999 a number of soup kitchens have been operating in Poole, with a different local church taking a responsibility for each evening of the week. Whilst the official count of rough sleepers for the town is just two, typically each evening would see ten to twenty people attending. Not all are rough sleepers, but all are vulnerable and at the margins of society because of mental health issues, drug or alcohol addictions, unemployment or criminal convictions etc. Though this work provides an important link with such groups of people, by itself it could legitimately be criticised for making life comfortable for its clients where they are, rather than promoting and encouraging change. So in April 2004 Faithworks Poole appointed a part-time outreach worker to support those attending the soup kitchens in getting access to health care, acquiring jobs and finding secure housing. This post is funded primarily by the local Drug Action Team (DAT), and is directly a consequence of a relationship that has been forged between the DAT and Faithworks Poole.

On the face of it, this project arose out of discussions between the manager of Faithworks Poole and the contracts manager of the DAT. Both had previously worked with each other, however, and had built a relationship in social services over several years. The DAT were initially asked to provide input into a training event for soup kitchen volunteers one Saturday morning. Provision of soup and rolls is fine, but information on the range of statutory services is critical if volunteers are to link rough sleepers with the right skilled professionals successfully. Having contributed to the training day, Faithworks Poole then approached the contracts manager of the DAT with a simple request: 'How about going 50/50 on funding an outreach worker?' There were no formal letters, no completion of application forms, and no being pulled from pillar to post by local government bureaucracy. Rather an existing relationship was unashamedly utilised in order to meet the shared aim of seeing people's lives change. Within a week of the request, the DAT agreed to a partnership through the provision of £20,000 over two years, along with full support for the Faithworks employee (who came from one of the local churches) through their inclusion within the Drug Action Team's established induction and training programmes.

Here are some practical steps you might consider in working to build strong and healthy relationships:

1   Make the first move – look for ways in which you can make the other person's job easier or more enjoyable and act on them.
2   Act, don't say – be aware that what you say about yourself or what you can offer will be treated with suspicion. The best way to demonstrate that you have something to contribute is to start contributing.
3   Listen to what the other person has to say.
4   Ask questions.
5   Don't rush in with easy answers – earn the right to offer advice.
6   Say what you mean.
7   Ask for help when you need it.
8   Be consistent.
9   Apologise when you make a mistake.

Self Interest

If trust is built through a combination of credibility, dependability and relationship, it is always damaged by self interest. The simple truth is that however hard you try to build trust, if you give the impression that you are in the relationship for what you can get out of it, your efforts will be in vain. The used car salesman who asks to be trusted faces a massive uphill struggle. His self interest in gaining the maximum profit from the car he's trying to sell is a huge barrier to trust. We all view television adverts in a completely different way to current affairs programmes – adverts are trying to sell us something and, though they often try to be entertaining or informative, their ulterior motive is still very clear. We are not easily fooled.

For the Church, self interest is just as much of a problem as it is for the business world. One of the great barriers to successful partnership, not to mention funding bids, is the belief that the Church is involved simply to win converts – that getting 'bums on seats' is our chief, indeed our only, real concern. If we are to be trusted providers of social welfare, proselytism cannot be our agenda, hidden or otherwise. In the same way that most people wouldn't be comfortable if government funds were being used to generate converts to Islam, Christian proselytism is guaranteed to kill trust. (For more on this see the section on the Faithworks Charter, p. 90)

Of course, everyone has a degree of self interest – that's understood and accepted. So the real question is how committed are we to a 'win win' relationship? How much will we genuinely work for the 'win' of our partner? Dealing with anyone who is fundamentally as interested in your agenda as in their own is an amazing experience. As a wise man once said, 'There is no end to what you can achieve in life, so long as you don't care who gets the credit.' Or as Jesus himself put it, 'Love your neighbour as you love yourself.'

Self Interest – A Faithworks Case Study

Faithworks Poole has trustees and employees drawn from across the town's churches. It is non-denominational. It does not get involved in theological or doctrinal debate, but rather provides opportunities for a broad spectrum of Christians to demonstrate their faith in direct practical ways. Its only 'self interest' then is in promoting the Christian faith in ways that support and complement the work of the local government and other voluntary bodies. Thus, rather than seeing Faithworks as threatening or conflicting with their interests, the council view them positively. The resulting partnership enables them to demonstrate in practical terms how they relate to and engage with the local faith communities.

Though 'partnership' and 'joined up thinking' are the buzz words for local government officers, engaging with faith communities can be a complex issue. Faithworks Poole has, therefore, provided the council and the Local Strategic Partnership with the framework for achieving their goal. So, though Faithworks have benefited hugely, they have also genuinely contributed in helping local government fulfil a pressing agenda.

You can make sure that you don't appear self interested by taking some of the following steps.

1   Ask the person you are dealing with to talk about what, for them, are the concerns behind the given issue.
2   Ask your partners, or potential partners, lots of open-ended questions.

3   Focus on defining their problems with them rather than prematurely guessing at possible solutions.
4   Listen to, and remember, what is said – comment at the end rather than jumping in with your suggestions.
5   Don't relate everything to you and your situation.
6   Give visual and verbal clues that you are listening and understanding what is being said to you.

Adding it All Up

So

$$\text{Trust} = \frac{\text{Credibility} + \text{Dependability} + \text{Relationship}}{\text{Self Interest}}$$

But we can go further. If we assign values (0-10) to the different parts of the equation it is easy to begin to see the difference that trust makes in a situation. A good friend, for example, might regard you as being highly credible and give you a score of 8 out of 10 for this. Because he has known you a long time he has learnt that you don't often let him down and so would mark you as a 7 for dependability. He also feels that your relationship is strong and might give you 9 out of 10 for this. Over time he has been able to appreciate that you have often supported him in chasing and achieving his goals and, therefore, he believes you are not self-centred. Therefore he awards you a low mark for self interest. So the trust equation looks like this:

$$T = \frac{8 + 7 + 9}{3} = T = \frac{24}{3} = \text{Trust Level} = 8$$

In a new relationship, however, where you've not yet had the chance to prove your credibility or dependability, where you don't have a strong relationship and the other person can't really know that you're not just trying to get something out of them, then the trust equation might look more like this:

$$T = \frac{5+4+5}{7} = T = \frac{14}{7} = \text{Trust Level} = 2$$

This isn't a scientific process, but it is a good indication of the way in which credibility, dependability, relationship and self interest will always determine the level to which you are trusted.

The Four Stages of Learning

Trust is about sincerity but it's also about technique. Some people worry about this endlessly and beat themselves up constantly about their motives in any relationship. However, the truth is that it is usually easier to act your way into right thinking than it is to think your way into right acting. We all suffer from mixed motives and constantly question ourselves, but the best way of dealing with this is to engage, not withdraw. It might sound cynical to say 'fake it till you make it', but the truth is that we need to be intentional about the way we interact with people until it becomes second nature.

There are four stages of human learning:

1 Unconscious incompetence
2 Conscious incompetence
3 Conscious competence
4 Unconscious competence

When we start out at something, we often don't even have enough knowledge or skill to discern that we are incompetent at it (unconscious incompetence). However, as we learn more, we eventually become aware of our previously unrecognised incompetence. This Eureka moment is the dawning of conscious incompetence. And, though it is depressing, it really is a giant breakthrough because it is only this recognition that can provide us with the springboard to grow, learn and develop. If we then work at learning the appropriate skills, we eventually reach a level at which, though it's not easy, we begin to put our weaknesses behind us. This is stage three – conscious competence –and it is hard work because we have to keep thinking in order to deliver. But when we stick at it, gradually the highest level of learning develops (unconscious competence), when we don't have to worry about what we are doing and even begin to find ourselves doing it, without thinking, by second nature.

If you have ever tried to learn to juggle you will be very familiar with this process. At first you might throw the balls and catch them in a random order – you might even say at this point that you can, in fact, juggle naturally. However, if you watch anyone who really can juggle, you soon realise that you can't! There is a specific pattern to their throws and catches, something that you cannot yet emulate. After a few hours' practice, you might be able to juggle in the correct way for a short period, provided of course you are really concentrating very hard on what you are doing. Eventually, though, if you keep practising you will reach a level of proficiency at which you don't even have to think about the balls you are throwing and catching – you can carry on a conversation with someone while you're juggling and even make eye contact with them, without dropping a single ball. Juggling has become a background activity that you can now do even while your mind is elsewhere.

It's exactly the same with our efforts to build trust. At first we might not even realise how badly we have been performing. Sometimes it takes a big shock to draw us up short. But over time and with a lot of hard work, we can not only develop the behaviour patterns that help to build trust, but eventually we no longer even have to think about our techniques – they gradually become the natural way in which we enact our sincerity.

> *'A man who doesn't trust himself can never really trust anyone else.'*
>
> Cardinal De Retz

Before we move on, however, the deepest and most challenging truth is this. Whether we are talking about building trust in churches or governments, businesses or royal families, eventually it all comes down to the same, and far more personal, issue. Though healthy institutions of the future must find behaviours and policies which demonstrate their credibility, dependability, open and transparent relationships and lack of self interest, in the end all this boils down to not so much the behaviour and trustworthiness of the institutions themselves, but that of the individuals who comprise them.

Three

Can the Church Trust the Government?

'I have learnt that politicians won't be respected by the public unless they respect each other and people won't trust us unless we trust them.'

Michael Howard

The idea of 'Equal Opportunities' has been around for many years. The first Equal Opportunities legislation was born in the aftermath of the two world wars. Thousands of British men and women were left disabled by their involvement in the conflicts and, despite losing limbs for King and country, were often discriminated against when it came to finding employment. The various ex-service men and women's associations lobbied to have the right to be considered for employment in spite of disability enshrined in law. Eventually the Disabled Persons (Employment) Act was passed in 1944. The cry went up 'We are all equal – we are all the same!' The voice of the people had been heard and addressed in law.

Twenty years later, it became apparent that black and other ethnic minority communities in Britain were also experiencing widespread discrimination and the term 'Equal Opportunities' was taken up by the champions of racial equality. Eventually in 1965 the Race Relations Act was passed to ensure that ethnic minorities had the same rights of access to housing and public services as the white majority. The Act, in theory at least, made it illegal to discriminate against someone on the grounds of their ethnicity.

In the same vein, the 1970s saw more legislation passed. This time it focused on gender issues, in a determined effort to offer parity to women in employment, both in terms of the work they could undertake and their fair and equal remuneration for that work. The cry was heard again, 'We are all equal – we are all the same!'

But in truth, none of this legislation had very much impact. In fact, it wasn't until the Greater London Council (GLC) adopted tough measures to combat the inequalities in employment (including the requirement that all organisations that wanted to be considered for funding must have an Equal Opportunities policy) that real change began to bite.

As a result of this, the climate surrounding Equal Opportunities began at last to improve. Over time, other local authorities began to adopt similar approaches and gradually both private and public sector employers began to see the value in bringing themselves in line. Within a very short space of time, Equal Opportunities had changed from being an easily ignored abstract concept to a very real, high-profile fact of life, delivering justice to many who were shut out from it in the past.

Then, in the 1990s, an important new concept began to emerge – equality and diversity. Many people still think that 'equality and diversity' is simply Equal Opportunities in a shiny new suit – nothing, they think, has really changed. But far from being a new term for an old concept, equality and diversity represents an urgent new cry for a new generation – 'We are all equal, but we are *not* the same. We are all different!'

As part of this new direction, in December 2003 a new law came into effect in the UK (except Northern Ireland) to safeguard the employment rights of people, regardless of their faith; a law that makes it illegal to consider a person's religious beliefs when recruiting staff. The Employment Equality Regulations (Religion and Belief) do, however, contain the caveat that a person's faith can be taken into account if there is a 'genuine occupational requirement' (GOR) for a potential employee to hold certain religious beliefs. Of course, though the terminology is new, the concept behind genuine occupational requirements is an old one – it would be difficult to imagine an employment tribunal being held over a theatre director's insistence that, in a production of *To Kill a Mockingbird*, Atticus Finch should be played by a white man and the actor taking the role of Tom Robinson should be black!

Though many churches saw the new law in a negative light and a few Christian agencies presented it as a catastrophe, in truth, the issue of equality and diversity actually presents the Church with a huge opportunity. The right of churches, Christian projects and faith agencies in general to employ people who share their beliefs is now enshrined in law. The voice of the people has been heard 'We are all equal, but we are *not* the same. We are all different!' The Church's question to government is now simply this: 'Do you understand the implications of your own policy? If you do, it's time to let real change bite.'

Fruit Salad or Fruit Purée

It was not uncommon during the 1960s and beyond to hear white supporters of the civil rights movement in the

United States claiming to be colour-blind. Their meaning was clear. They were saying, along with Martin Luther King Jr in the words of his famous 'I have a dream' speech of 28 August 1963, that people should 'not be judged by the colour of their skin but by the content of their character'. However, though this stance was vitally important within the context of the civil rights struggle, it was a short-term approach. Someone afflicted with colour-blindness is, in fact, the poorer for it. They are robbed of a great joy. A beautiful photograph, containing many colours and hues, is reduced to the dull monochrome of black and white and shades of grey. The delicate nuances and subtle alterations in colour are surely to be celebrated, not destroyed. The manufacturers of computers are always keen to boast about the number of colours their machines can display. The first computer I ever used showed everything in two shades – green or black. This soon developed into eight colours, then sixteen, then thirty-two – and today millions. The more that subtle differences are recognised, the more lifelike a picture becomes.

In many ways the Equal Opportunities agenda before the 1990s was pushing for colour-blindness. Employers were encouraged to disregard ethnicity, gender and physical abilities – everyone was to be considered the same. Blandness was the order of the day. The culinary equivalent of Equal Opportunities would be puréeing mixed fruit in a blender – all of the constituent parts are present, but it becomes impossible to discern any individual colours, forms or flavours. What you end up with is all boringly exactly the same.

The great strength of the emerging concept of equality and diversity is that, rather than lumping us all together and viewing each individual as being no different from anyone else, our differences are to be celebrated, not obliterated. Equality and diversity recognises that we are not all the same; we are unique. This new 'fruit salad' attitude towards equality is far more positive. In a fruit salad each individual piece of fruit retains its unique characteristics while, at the same time, the different fruits mix and enhance one another. The sharpness of pineapple is offset by the sweetness of pear; the smoothness of banana contrasts with the citrus bite of orange.

In exactly the same way it is ludicrous to suggest that all people are the same, that each race, ethnic or interest group bears the same characteristics and that there is no difference between the genders. Diversity is about acknowledging not only that we are all different, but also that, when we embrace those differences, together we make a stronger society.

> *'Diversity is founded on the premise that harnessing the differences will create a productive environment in which everyone feels valued, where their talents are being fully utilised and in which organisational goals are met.'*
>
> Pearn Kandola

Of course, the same is true for faith groups – we cannot be lumped together in one category, indistinguishable from one another. The truth is that equality and diversity has huge ramifications for government, the Church and other faith groups. In many ways even government has been slow to recognise the implications of its own policy. The 'faith-sector' does not exist. That rather unfortunate and short-sighted government term, often used nowadays in an attempt to create some kind of umbrella reference to Christians, Muslims, Jews, Sikhs, Hindus and others, is not only a misnomer, it flies in the face of the government's own legislation. The new law is about equality and diversity – not equality and uniformity. For the Church, our faith is in Jesus. He is our engine, our motivation, not some nebulous concept of all-embracing faith. The new legislation should actually serve to protect our diversity and free us to maintain our distinctive qualities. The challenge to each department of government, then, is this: Can we trust you to stand by the spirit of your legislation, not just allowing us to remain distinctive but celebrating that distinctiveness? This is an issue of credibility and dependability. Will you deliver on your promise or is it empty?

> *'This party will, ultimately, be judged on its ability to deliver on its promises.'*
>
> Tony Blair

No Faith, No Works

Each year the broadsheets publish a list of the nation's schools indicating how well each is performing. At the beginning of 2004, these school league tables reported the fact that faith-based schools were out-performing their secular counterparts – pupils are, it seems, likely to get a better education if the school they attend has a basis of faith. In fact, this is not news. Both government and parents have long recognised the value of church and other faith-based schools.

> *'Faith-based schools are a pillar of the education system valued by very many parents for their faith character, their moral emphasis and the high quality of education they generally provide.'*
>
> Tony Blair

What the government has more difficulty in identifying, it would seem, is why faith-based schools are performing so well. In his former role as Education Secretary, David Blunkett was reported as saying that he wanted to 'bottle' the ethos of faith schools. The outcome of the discussion was a proposal for a project designed to see if it was possible to recreate the positive learning environment of a faith-based school but without the basis of faith. As far as I am aware, the project never materialised – and it's not hard to see why.

It seems unbelievable that the generally excellent performance of church schools and other faith-based organisations should be so mysterious to the government. Trying to capture the achievements of these projects without the basis of faith that undergirds them is bound to be fruitless. The simple truth is that, as uncomfortable as it might be for some to accept, it is faith itself that provides the results that the government are so keen to emulate. The reason Christian schools and community projects deliver is because they are Christian. This is the essence of their success: it is not an 'incidental'! And if the government doubt it, why don't they field test it?

Oasis Trust, the charity which I started twenty years ago, has accomplished many things. In this country we have offered healthcare to thousands of homeless people in London. We have given hundreds of young homeless people a chance to get off the streets, helping them to rebuild their lives and move on as positive and productive members of society. We have helped drug addicts and alcoholics to break free of their addictions. We have given training opportunities to the long-term unemployed. And, through Faithworks, we have encouraged countless local churches to further their engagement with their communities. Worldwide we have set up hospitals, schools and training schemes helping people to learn a trade; we have taught people to purify water, heal their sick children, earn money, raise their aspirations and discover hope. And why have we done all of this? Simply because of our faith in Jesus who commands us to love our neighbour as ourselves!

The truth is that, were it not for our faith, we wouldn't do our job at all. For Christians, our faith in Christ is our motivation, our heart, our engine and our strength. I cannot count the number of times that I have seen my colleagues at Oasis working late into the night, ignoring the limits of their contract of employment, so that they might get a job done to a high quality in a limited time. This happens for one reason and for one reason alone, because not only are they working for Oasis, they are working for God – our work is simply an expression of our faith in, and commitment to, Jesus Christ. And our Christian faith not only motivates us to work hard and to work well, it means that we keep going when others might give up – we are in it for the long haul.

For any government, national or local, to sideline faith and focus solely on accomplishments is therefore naïve in the extreme. You simply cannot expect to get the results of a faith-based organisation without faith, any more than you can have a sandwich without bread. Government is perfectly happy to praise our work, but will never really understand us until they grasp the critical role that our faith in Jesus plays. For the Church at least, no faith, no works!

Our challenge to government, then, is simple. Accept that our faith in Christ is the motivation for all that we do. Recognise that, even though you might not understand it; it is the key ingredient of our work and without it we will not function. Don't make it difficult for us to remain distinctively Christian without then expecting those difficulties to affect the impact and quality of our work. Celebrate our faith – don't knock it. Turn the concept of equality and diversity into a living reality.

A Level Playing Field

> *'I believe the Lib Dems can offer real solutions to the country's problems. Why? Because our kind of politics is based in trust and fairness.'*
> Charles Kennedy

Central government is, on paper, very happy to recognise the value of faith communities. They are aware that the Church, Christian organisations and other faith groups deliver millions of pounds' worth of social welfare care each year. For instance, they acknowledge that the Church does more youth work than any other voluntary agency, and that the social ills of homelessness, drug abuse and alcoholism would be totally unmanageable were it not for the continued work of faith-based initiatives. But in fact, the Church's situation is even more dynamic than is often recognised. It is not until you factor in the number of individual Christian volunteers working separately for secular charities (the Samaritans, Relate, ChildLine and thousands of smaller local entities) that you begin to gain a true perspective of the scale of the Church's overall energy and activity. However, though government realises that if the ongoing community work of local churches was withdrawn much of the social infrastructure of the UK would soon grind to a halt, and while they are more than happy to work *with* faith-based organisations, in practice what they often mean is something subtly different from that – they are happy to accept the work *of* faith groups, but not their faith.

Scarcely a week passes in the Faithworks office without one of our team receiving a phone call from a local church or group of churches who have felt discriminated against in a bid for local government funding or recognition. Of course, there are many occasions when funding is rightly turned down. Some Christian projects, for instance, lack the professionalism or clear, targeted goals and outcomes that the use of taxpayers' money demands. However, we can cite numerous occasions in which funding applications from churches or Christian organisations have been turned down, simply and even explicitly, for no other reason than the fact that they were from Christians. Similarly, from time to time, we receive calls asking us, in effect, how to submit a funding application for vital community work without making it too clear that the project in question has a basis of faith. This is clearly a problem as it tempts Christian groups to be less than transparent about their motives and, in so doing, threatens to undermine their faith and trustworthiness through their dilution or even denial.

The greatest tactic to counteract the discrimination the Church faces is, of course, to deliver such high-quality work that the 'problem' of our faith is overcome. Recently Oasis UK's Community Action department entered an unusual competition. One of the London borough councils offered a disused pub called 'The Rising Sun' to anyone with a good plan to turn it into a useful community facility. Oasis put in a bid for the property. Eventually we were short-listed, but then were explicitly told that our faith made it unlikely that we would win – in fact we were told that we shouldn't even have entered! Ultimately, however, the strength of our plan to turn the building into an enterprise centre, providing vocational training and business start-up support to young people in the surrounding community, meant that we were successful and were awarded the pub. Despite the fact that the odds were stacked against us, the quality of our work meant that we were successful. It is for this reason that Faithworks produces many resources to help churches and Christian charities deliver truly high-quality services.

> *'The more I want to get something done, the less I call it work.'*
>
> Richard Bach

The fact remains, though, that while we can still be successful if we work hard and deliver the best business plans, we shouldn't have to fight against discrimination. It is true that the Church needs to work hard to ensure that it achieves a level of professionalism equal to its secular counterparts, but it should not have to do more than this. Funding applications should not be an uphill struggle simply because of our faith.

Central government's own legislation on equality and diversity should serve to protect our right to be different – to be distinctively Christian. But this legislation will only come of age when Christian bids for local government funding are considered on the same footing as any other applications. What we are asking for is really very simple – a genuine, UK-wide, level playing field for both the work of faith groups and the faith that inspires it. We welcome the new law protecting equality in the face of religious diversity, just as we welcomed the government's 2001 election manifesto promise of a level playing field. But promises are not enough. We need to know that government can be trusted both to understand fully the implications of its own legislation and then to act consistently on them and deliver.

Equality and diversity is a much-loved agenda of government, both nationally and locally – it makes for great rhetoric. However, it is critical that the government recognises that any true commitment to equality must always actively embrace a real understanding of diversity. Where discrimination remains against faith groups this commitment simply falls by the wayside, and with it equality collapses. If the Church has to down play its faith in order to gain partnership or financial support for its work, it has surrendered its diversity and the law has failed.

Expressed simply, we don't want special treatment because of our faith. We are not asking to be given funding because we are Christians, but neither should we be denied it for that reason. All we want is a fair system, which actually works at the local level, in which partnership and funds (where appropriate) are awarded to the best projects – whatever their religious beliefs. So where the secular humanists are delivering, fund them! Only then can any government really be said to be working with faith groups.

Our message to local and national government is this. Treat us fairly and you can rely on us to deliver good results. Partner with us and we rise to the challenge. Fund our work and we will not let you down. Celebrate, endorse and support our diversity and offer us equality. Judge us on our merits, not on our beliefs. Only then will you prove that you believe in equality and diversity, rather than equality and uniformity.

Order in the House

One of the difficulties of dealing with large institutions is that uniformity cannot be guaranteed. We recognise that the Church doesn't really have a party line on much except the death and resurrection of Jesus Christ. Different churches have different agendas, diverse outlooks and distinct understandings of their role in society. No single person or group can claim to be representative of the whole Church.

However, year on year, more and more diverse churches and Christian organisations are signing up to the Faithworks Charter, which provides a benchmark of professionalism for them as they serve their communities. (See p. 49). Together, without eroding our differences or independence of one another, we are developing an increasingly unified voice and standard of delivery. We are bringing our house in order.

We need to know that central government is also working to bring the same kind of common approach to local councils across the UK as they interpret and enact central government policy. As we explored earlier, the first laws protecting the rights of people with disabilities and ethnic minority groups were largely ignored until the Greater London Council enforced them. Only then did others follow. It is not enough for this to be the case with the equality and diversity legislation. How does central government intend to stimulate a greater understanding of, and commitment to, equality and diversity?

As the situation stands, different councils have different stances on partnership with, and the funding of, faith groups. Some are excellent and the new legislation will have little impact on them as they were celebrating diversity and offering equality long before the law was passed. However, in other places there is still great cause for concern. Central government needs to address the question of how it will ensure equal treatment of churches and other faith groups, regardless of their location. It must be unacceptable to leave the application of the law to chance; and it is a flagrant denial of the law for different local authorities to be allowed to adopt different policies and get away with it.

Our plea to government is this: 'How will you ensure that the law on equality and diversity is the same, in practice as on paper, in every local council area of the UK? How will you ensure that all local councils in the UK tow the line? How will you go about making the playing field genuinely level in every area of the UK? What will you do to bring rogue councils into line? The cry has gone up "We are all equal, but we are *not* all the same. We are different!" Have you heard us?'

Four

Can the Government Trust the Church?

'Admitting error might be one way to restore trust.'
Rowan Williams

If you point your finger at someone else, three more point straight back at you! As the Church challenges government to create a level playing field and work with the distinctiveness of our faith, we too have challenges to face. If we want to be trusted, we need to demonstrate our trustworthiness. For us, just as for government, the trust of the public is built on our credibility, our dependability, the quality and depth of our relationships and our lack of self interest. In order for this to happen, we need to work hard to overcome the suspicion that Christian welfare provision is simply proselytism via the backdoor; that our churches are self-serving and often detached from the real needs of the communities of which they are supposed to be part; and that what we do is short term and amateurish. We need to demonstrate we are already in the forefront of 'hands-on' community welfare across the UK and are now keen to build our capacity and deliver excellent and sustainable, life-changing models of care.

That's what the Faithworks Charter is all about – a radical manifesto designed to offer principles on which to build the Church's trustworthiness. If we are going to work in our communities and in partnership with other agencies and local and national government, then we need to be committed to doing so in a professional and trustworthy manner.

Put together by a team of professionals including practitioners, church leaders, lawyers and policy makers, the Faithworks Charter offers an aspirational 'benchmark' for local churches, Christian agencies and projects to sign up to and then work hard towards. Already hundreds of churches and Christian organisations around the UK are discovering that they slowly build trust within their local communities and with local government when they commit themselves to achieving the standards of the Faithworks Charter. And as thousands more churches of all denominations along with Christian community projects and agencies stand together to deliver this standard of excellence, our goal is that Christ's Church will begin to be taken just as seriously as a key welfare provider of the twenty-first century as we were in centuries past.

Unpacking the Faithworks Charter

What follows is an unpacking of the individual clauses of the Faithworks charter – setting out the principles which build trust by demonstrating the trustworthiness of local churches and Christian projects. Your church, Christian organisation or project can become a Faithworks affiliate by signing the Faithworks charter. (For more information and a full copy of the charter see p. 90.)

THE FAITHWORKS CHARTER

PRINCIPLES FOR CHURCHES AND LOCAL CHRISTIAN AGENCIES COMMITTED TO EXCELLENCE IN COMMUNITY WORK AND SERVICE PROVISION IN THE UK

Motivated by our Christian faith we commit ourselves to serve others by aspiring to the following standards in all our community work.

We will provide an inclusive service to our community by:

1   *Serving and respecting all people regardless of their gender, marital status, race, ethnic origin, religion, age, sexual orientation or physical and mental capacity.*

Equality – regarding people as equal and therefore treating them equally is fundamental to Christianity. As Christians, we believe that each person possesses a basic dignity that comes from being made 'in the image of God', rather than from any human quality or accomplishment, their race or gender, age or economic status.

Diversity – acknowledging that God made us all as unique and different beings – is also a central tenet of Christian belief. Indeed, from a Christian point of view, we believe that diversity is the basis of equality.

So for churches and Christian projects, serving and respecting all people, regardless of who they are, is really just about putting our theology of equality and diversity into practice. However, this goes well until, as service providers or employers, we are asked to operate according to standards which clash with our own understanding of what is right and wrong. For example, as a social landlord, we may be asked to provide hostel accommodation in a double room to a couple who are partners but who are not married or, as a community centre, we may be asked to hire out a room to a different faith group to meet and pray in our building.

Clearly, in these situations and many others, churches and Christian projects have a choice about what to do. One approach is to say 'No' to these requests in order to avoid diluting our identity as Christians – 'If we allow these things to happen we are not being true to the Christian purpose of our work.'

However, an alternative is to turn the situation around – to look at how we can maintain, even strengthen, our Christian identity, by serving the needs of these people. Allowing those who are not the same as us to have access to a service which we offer does not mean that we agree with their way of life or that we cannot promote our own way of life. Equally, limiting access to a service to those in need of it can be interpreted as anything but Christian.

Jesus never made the support and care he offered conditional. People did not have to change before he met their needs. He served them regardless of who they were or where they came from.

2   *Acknowledging the freedom of people of all faiths or none both to hold and to express their beliefs and convictions respectfully and freely, within the limits of the UK law.*

There are two pieces of UK legislation on religion and belief. The Charter for Human Rights states that individuals have the right to practise their religion and the recent employment legislation on equality and diversity (see p. 35) is designed to outlaw discrimination in the work-place on the grounds of religion or belief.

So what impact does all this have? Many churches and Christian organisations run hostels for homeless people, including refugees. One particular hostel decides to take in a Muslim family who, during their stay, wish to have a place identified for prayer. The hostel already provides a chapel for personal prayer and reflection but this is not appropriate for the needs of the Muslims. This hostel may feel that the provision of this space is to deny the Christian basis of the work of the hostel. On the other hand, such an approach may technically be in breach of the Muslim residents' human rights to express their religious beliefs. So here we have a situation of the rights of one faith against the rights of another. As in the case of most human rights matters, it is unclear how the Charter for Human Rights would legislate on this.

However, regardless of the scope of the Charter for Human Rights, surely as Christians we would not wish to rely on legislation to determine the right course of action. Providing the prayer space does not have to be seen to be a denial of our Christian faith but more as an act of service *because* of our Christian faith. The outcome is not so much a dilution of our faith but more an enhancement of it. Real confidence in our Christian identity comes when we begin to depend less for our identity on those things which make us look like Christians. The Church has often spent too much time worrying about how it looks rather than what it actually is.

Moving onto the other area of UK law, we come now to the most recent employment legislation, introduced in December 2003. Officially known as the Employment Equality Regulations (Religion and Belief), this legislation is designed to prevent employers discriminating against employees on the grounds of religion and belief, unless such discrimination can be justified. In essence, what the law says is that employers cannot treat people of faith less favourably than those of no faith.

But, though this is good news for all those people of faith in secular employment, when it comes to faith groups that act as employers, it has appeared on first reading, to some, to cause major problems. This is because it is designed to prevent discrimination on the grounds of religion and belief which is, of course, the very thing that an employer of a faith-based organisation wants to do in order maintain their distinctive faith identity. However, in order to accommodate the needs of religious organisations, the law does allow religious discrimination to take place but only where this can be justified as a genuine occupational requirement (GOR) which is 'in accordance with the religious ethos of the organisation'.

Faithworks has developed a 'Christian Ethos Audit' pack which is designed to help Christian employers identify their ethos and then make their employment decisions in line with it. It is available on-line from www.faithworks.info or from the Faithworks office.

3 Never imposing our Christian faith or belief on others.

In Matthew 28:18–20, Jesus commands the eleven disciples 'to go and make disciples of all nations, baptising them in the name of the Father, the Son and the Holy Spirit and teaching them to obey everything I have commanded you'. The instructions are very clear – and they don't add 'but be careful not to impose your Christian faith on others'.

So putting the Great Commission side by side with this clause of the Faithworks Charter raises some significant questions. If we sign up to the Charter, are we signing away our rights to make disciples, to bring people into the Christian faith and to hand on the message of Jesus?

Jesus respected the freedom of all those with whom he came into contact. He responded to their needs: sometimes he offered advice or a challenge about the way they should live in the future but he never forced himself or his world-view on them – or made them some kind of 'offer they couldn't refuse'!

This clause of the Faithworks Charter does not imply that we should shrink back from expressing our faith in whatever service we are offering to the public. Quite to the contrary, we need to celebrate our Christian identity and maintain and promote it in whatever activity we are engaged. It simply says that we should not use our public service as a back door to proselytising (attempting to force others to convert) or an opportunity to harangue others about our faith – neither of which ever work anyway.

4   *Developing partnerships with other churches, voluntary groups, statutory agencies and local government wherever appropriate in order to create an effective, integrated service for our clients avoiding unnecessary duplication of resources.*

Building partnerships in the delivery of public services enables each organisation involved to work to their strengths and thus together to be able to create solutions which are more effective and reliable for their clients.

However, developing partnership can sound like a great idea for any organisation until reality sets in. And the stakes are even higher for the church or Christian organisation which may consider partnership with secular agencies and, to be honest, even other churches or Christian organisations, as a threat to their distinctive identity. So how do we do this without losing that identity?

When churches or Christian organisations deliver services in response to community need, in some ways the programmes of work will not *look* very different from the work delivered by non-Christian agencies. However, while it may not *look* different, we do need to be clear about the way in which it *is* different. Otherwise there is little point in sticking out for the right of Christians to deliver public services and to have a level playing field on which to do it in the first place.

The 'Christ-centred' difference lies, very often wholly, in the motivation with which the work is undertaken. Clearly, while this motivation may not affect the actual shape of the work delivered, i.e. what services are delivered, to whom and when etc., it will affect the way in which the work is delivered.

To be trusted and fulfilled in any partnership we need to be true to who we are. But, in order to do this and not allow a partnership with non-Christian partners to weaken our Christian identity we need to work out how to stay true to these values, not just in the work we deliver but also in our internal practices as a church or a Christian organisation.

The Faithworks *Christian Ethos Audit* is a helpful tool for this purpose, or contact the Faithworks office for information about further advice and training in this area.

5   *Providing and publicising regular consultation and reporting forums to client groups and the wider community regarding the effective development and delivery of our work and our responsiveness to their actual needs.*

The establishment of a local steering group is a good way for any project both to identify needs in consultation with the community and to help develop a reporting process about the delivery of its work. The purpose of such a group would be to ensure that your church or Christian project is delivering, wherever possible, to genuine local needs; that problems are worked out with people and not for them, and that plans for future services emerge out of the views of local people.

Your local steering group could include local people who already benefit from your services, e.g. tenants/residents, parents who attend the parent/toddler group, people who use social facilities and those who live locally but who so far have not found the services to be of benefit.

As an advisory group to the trustees (or any other governing body) the steering group would need to be treated seriously. There is little point in engaging them only to ignore their concerns and advice. It would be important to set out terms of reference that identified their management responsibility and the way in which they would relate to the trustees/decision makers. It might be useful to designate at least one member to be a co-opted trustee (i.e. be given an invitation to attend and contribute to trustees meetings) or for a trustee to become a member of this group.

We will value all individuals in a way that is consistent with our distinctive Christian Ethos by:

1   Creating an environment where clients, volunteers and employees are encouraged and enabled to realise their potential.

Jill Garrett, previously Executive Director for Gallup, claims that 'any given individual will be better than ten thousand others at one particular thing. All we have to do', she adds, 'is find out what that one thing is!' Discovering and realising what we are best at and, indeed, are better at than ten thousand others is about discovering and realising our potential.

Churches and Christian organisations have the chance to provide each individual with the opportunity that might never have been available or recognised at school, college or elsewhere – to enable them to explore and realise their potential.

Being made in the image of God, we all have God-given potential – which means that the commitment to enabling people to achieve their potential should form part of the ethos and values of every church project and Christian organisation. When people start to work within the area of their potential they will be far more productive. This is likely to be accompanied by an increase in energy because working in one's area of potential comes naturally to people and is not a strain.

So, given that it makes biblical and commercial sense to help people discover their area of potential, the question is how does a church or an organisation do this? The answer is to develop an organisation that is genuinely committed to its people and where the systems and procedures are designed not just to deliver a service but to facilitate people's personal development. This kind of culture does not happen by itself. It is essential that a formal commitment is made by those responsible for the project or organisation (perhaps even a policy developed to articulate the procedures) and, wherever possible, some financial investment, however small, is also made in order to demonstrate that commitment.

2   *Assisting our clients, volunteers and employees to take responsibility for their own learning and development, both through formal and informal training opportunities and ongoing assessment.*

'People who stop learning', said Charles Handy, 'stop living. The same is true of organisations.' In fact, if a church or project itself is not a learning organisation it is almost impossible to expect its clients, staff or volunteers to develop an attitude to their own development that is counter to the prevailing culture.

One of the many inhibitors to learning can be the cost of training programmes and courses. But remember that learning is not necessarily the same thing as training. Training might help you to do something but learning is about growing in understanding and the ability to change. Learning opportunities are available almost everywhere. Learning does not have to cost but it does have to be factored in to your project's life. Here's how:

Everyone is a learner – even the leader, the leadership team, the governing body or the elders and the church council. Indeed, leaders have a great deal of responsibility for setting the learning culture. If people can see that these people take learning seriously by having a learning plan, which they then stick to, it makes a big difference to their commitment to their own learning.

Reflection – This is about creating times and spaces on agendas not just to review how previous events went but what can be learned from them. Then it's a case of noting your findings and bringing them forward to your next appropriate planning meeting.

Every experience is a learning experience – Any process of reflection will be even more valuable if the activity that is being reflected on was approached as a learning experience in the first place. Again, this has a great deal to do with the culture set by the leaders – 'Let's do the very best we can but also learn from what does not go well.' This gives people permission to experiment and to do so without fear of the consequences, if things turn out not quite as planned.

Shared vision – This can never be dictated to people; it has to be owned. Building a shared picture of the future the team wishes to create is time-consuming but more likely to encourage team members to want to achieve it and to do so together.

Dialogue – Not just another word for discussion! This is about our capacity consciously to suspend our own understanding and assumptions about others and enter into a genuine process of thinking together – one of respecting and pursuing people's contributions.

Organisations and people who have a learning approach to life will naturally help others to look at life in the same way. By creating this kind of environment we automatically enable our clients, volunteers and employees to take responsibility for their own learning and development.

3   Developing an organisational culture in which individuals learn from any mistakes made and where excellence and innovation are encouraged and rewarded.

The 'Campaign For Learning' definition of a learning organisation is one that benefits from the full brainpower, knowledge and experience of all its people to make sense of the world. It consciously transforms itself in its search for excellence. It actively encourages the learning of all individuals who work for it and with it, at the same time as implementing systems to ensure that the organisation is itself a learner. The working environment of a learning organisation is high challenge, low threat.

But what is an organisation of high challenge and low threat? An organisation that threatens is one that does not tolerate mistakes. But, given that mistakes are an inevitability, a low threat organisation is a realistic one that deals with them well. There is no point in suffering all the pain of making a mistake if we are not prepared to learn from it. The only question is how best to do this.

No one likes making mistakes but when we are punished for them, all we learn is to fear making them and therefore to stick to tried and tested methods rather than dare to experiment with what is new. A blame culture in an organisation always results in habits that stifle innovation, creativity and continuous improvement; it leads to an acceptance of the status quo; and the promotion of individual interests at the expense of the team.

Of course, some mistakes are very serious and threaten the viability of the whole organisation. But the danger is to treat all mistakes as if they were life threatening. Such an attitude will inevitably prevent significant learning. Bill Gates claims that he prefers to hire people who have made mistakes and faced up to them because the way a person deals with things when they go wrong is the best indicator of their inner strength and quality.

4   *Promoting the value of a balanced, holistic lifestyle as part of each individual's personal development.*

Our role as service providers is to add real quality, well-being and value to people's lives. Some examples might be:

Helping people to live independent lives – No matter how often you help someone who is homeless to find shelter you will not help them to solve their problems if you do not help them to deal with the issues that caused their situation in the first place. Supporting people with addiction, family breakdown or other problems that may be the cause of homelessness can be the first step on the road to independent living. Once these issues have been addressed, people can move onto vocational and life skills training that will slowly help them into greater independence.

Helping people to feel part of their local community – People who are shy or lack self esteem often feel isolated. Helping them to become part of a group in which they can experience support and acquire life skills will enable them slowly to develop a sense of belonging.

Helping people to improve their education and gain qualifications – Those who, for whatever reason, did not complete their education or gain qualifications and as a result are unable to gain regular employment can end up dropping out of society altogether. Social, personal and vocational skills are essential for increasing employability and a sense of responsibility and accountability as a citizen.

Helping people with difficult relationships – When relationships break down the consequences can be devastating for all parties involved. Helping people to deal with conflict with other family members, friends, partners or colleagues can restore a feeling of well being in their lives. The core of Jesus' life transforming message, though often deeply misunderstood, is that the Kingdom of God is good news for everyone, available at every stage of life.

5   *Abiding by the requirements of employment law in the UK and implementing best employment practices and procedures designed to maintain our distinctive ethos and values.*

It is often assumed that, because we are Christians, working relationships will be naturally and effortlessly filled with perpetual harmony. However, as we all know, life is not as simple as that. We all have different personal expectations and understandings that provide an ideal breeding ground for misunderstandings and conflict. The employment area is a classic area for such misunderstandings because it is so complex. Therefore, proper management is essential. There are two ways in which we can address this:

1 Fair procedures give employees a sense of justice and also enable employers to operate within the law. The following list of employment procedures enables employers to implement best practice:

- Equal Opportunities policy and procedures.
- Recruitment policy and procedures.
- Job descriptions.
- Terms and conditions of employment.
- Induction and work reviews.
- Standards and disciplinary procedures.
- Appeal, grievance and complaint procedures.

2 The Christian ethos of our project or organisation identifies what makes us different from other projects doing the same work.

- Being a Christian organisation is first and foremost about coming to terms with the fact that projects/organisations are made up of 'human beings' and not 'human doings'. If we believe that people are created by God, with God-given purpose, then our processes for recruitment and ongoing development need to reflect this fundamental fact.
- Opportunities for spiritual renewal and refreshment should also feature in our organisation's

people processes. Time away from the workplace does not have to be overlong or expensive but is an essential way to re-energise and re-focus the all important motivation which fuels the work.

Further information and guidelines for implementation in many of the areas mentioned above can be found in the book *Faithworks: Unpacked*, and the *Faithworks Christian Ethos Audit Pack* available from www.faithworks.info.

We will develop a professional approach to management, practice and funding by:

1   Implementing a management structure which fosters and encourages participation by staff at all levels in order to facilitate the fulfilment of the project's goals and visions.

Structures in any Christian project or agency should be, as in all effective organisations, governed by the need to achieve the mission. Most Christian projects or organisations are likely to be charities or charitable companies and are therefore subject to the requirements of charity law.

The management of a charity is influenced by the fact that:

- The trustees, who make up the Board of Management, hold the charity in trust and as such are ultimately responsible for its vision and mission.
- The Chief Executive has day-to-day operational responsibility for the delivery of this mission and is therefore accountable to the Board of Management reporting to its Chairperson.

The role of the board is to govern and the role of the staff is to manage. There is no clear-cut distinction between governance and management, though they should never overlap entirely. Instead, they need to be distinct but complementary.

Governance is the Board of Management's responsibility. It is concerned with:

- Ensuring that the organisation has a clear mission and strategy, but not necessarily with developing it.
- Ensuring that the organisation operates within the law and is well managed, but not necessarily with managing it.
- Giving guidance on the overall allocation of resources, but not necessarily with the precise numbers.
- Taking responsibility for the organisation's performance and long-term sustainability, but not necessarily with the detail of the performance measurement system.
- Providing insight, wisdom and good judgement, but leaving room for the staff to own and deliver the vision.

Management is a staff responsibility. Staff are responsible for:

- Supporting the process of developing strategy and for implementing it once it is agreed by the Board of Management.
- Turning the Board of Management's intentions into action.
- Administering the systems and procedures needed to get results.
- Helping ensure that the mechanics of the governance process run smoothly.

2   *Setting and reviewing measurable and timed outcomes
annually and regularly to evaluate and monitor our
management structure and output, recognising the need for
ongoing organisational flexibility, development and good
stewardship of resources.*

An organisation which is effective, efficient and respon-
sive to change is one in which:

- The purpose and mission of the organisation is known
  and understood – people do not have to think too hard
  to remember what the organisation exists to do. It is
  kept under regular review and is represented on all
  organisational literature.
- The three- or five-year strategy is developed out of an
  ongoing consultation process (both formal and informal) with staff and volunteers and therefore has wide
  ownership. It has strategic objectives and performance
  criteria attached to it, which are reviewed annually. The
  strategy includes a process of external review looking at
  key social, political, funding and economic trends as
  well as any significant technological developments
  likely to impact it.
- An annual plan is developed which relates closely to the
  longer-term strategy – it represents a step towards the
  achievement of the overall strategy and only includes
  plans which relate to that goal. The annual plan is
  costed and has supporting fund-raising plans.
- All staff members have job descriptions which flow
  from the targets set out in the strategy and annual plan.
  These are kept under regular review. When job changes
  occur, new job descriptions are written and agreed. The
  organisation encourages and supports staff to continue
  their personal and professional development so that
  they can meet and respond to the changing demands of
  the work.

- The organisation undertakes structural and mission reviews from time to time.

(See the book *Faithworks: Unpacked* – Sections 4.3, 4.6, 4.7)

3   *Doing all we can to ensure that we are not over-dependent on any one source of funding.*

Is your organisation financially viable or is it likely to collapse if one source of funding dries up? Achieving sustainability consists of two key components:

- Multi-source funding: almost every community project requires some level of start-up funding in order to get off the ground – and that usually comes from just one or two sources. However, a problem soon emerges when we don't diversify and instead allow our project to remain over-reliant on a small funding base. Single-source funding may appear to solve a headache but it actually makes any project hugely vulnerable. Only by working to develop a breadth of smaller grants or sources of income can we effectively avoid this 'dependency trap'.
- Financial self-sufficiency: the ideal situation for any social action project (or for that matter any business!) is financial self-sufficiency – generating income rather than relying on handouts, grants or subsidies. Though for many projects the goal of total self-sufficiency is an unrealisable dream, any and every step we can take towards it will necessarily increase our sustainability.

One way to go about this is moving from a dependence on grants to a position of being awarded contracts. Local and central government are increasingly 'contracting out' their services (e.g. youth work) and a growing number of Christian social action projects are successfully bidding for these. However, depending on the nature of your project, you might also be able to secure contracts from a range of other sources (e.g. paying customers). For example, an IT project which teaches unemployed people to use computers, might be forced to close if funding is withdrawn. However, a project that teaches IT skills in the context of its work as a professional web-design studio is much less vulnerable. There are a great number of social action projects which have managed to achieve a significant degree of financial self-sufficiency – the move from charity to enterprise – in this way.

4 Implementing best practice procedures in terms of Health and Safety and Child Protection in order to protect staff, volunteers and clients.

These policies and procedures are not red tape. They are essential to our success. Put bluntly, if we cannot demonstrate our intention to look after and protect people, we should not be in business. There are various model policies available in both these areas from a number of different sources. See the book *Faithworks: Unpacked* – section 5.9, or contact Faithworks at www.faithworks.info. However, the key to this issue is the implementation process. Having a policy agreed on paper means nothing until:

- Someone has responsibility for making sure the processes happen. This is about appointing Health and Safety and Child Protection Officers.
- The senior leaders/leadership team demonstrate, by their behaviour, that these matters are important to them and give their authority to the officers appointed to carry out the work.
- The role of the officers is clear, they are equipped to carry it out and staff, volunteers and management respect their authority.

- Budget and time have been made available for relevant training on these issues.
- The effect of the policies is monitored and reports are agenda items on quarterly/six-monthly meetings of the trustees/elders/senior management team.

5   Handling our funding in a transparent and accountable way and to give relevant people from outside our organisation/ project reasonable access to our accounts.

When funds are raised by the public, or public money is allocated to charities, the public has a right to know that the money is spent on those activities for which it was originally given. In the case of public spending bodies (e.g. health service, police, schools), there are regulators who act on our behalf to do this job. In the case of charities, the Charity Commission has this role.

As Christian charities we want to be able to demonstrate that we handle all our financial matters in a transparent and accountable way. This means that:

- Protocols are agreed for maximum spend, authorising cheque requisitions, payments by cheque or bank transfer, payroll entries, recruitment of new staff and agreeing new projects.
- Trustees/management are regularly provided with up-to-date accounts.
- Accounts are audited annually.
- Trustees are required to declare conflicts of interest and are not allowed to benefit financially or otherwise from their trustee role (e.g. to tender for work).
- Budgets are agreed on an annual basis.
- Staff/volunteers are held accountable to operate according to budget.
- Volunteers are reimbursed only according to receipted expenses.

- Restricted income (i.e. income given for any specific purpose) only supports that designated activity.
- Reserves are not used to fund activities which are not viable on an ongoing basis.

For further advice or training on how to implement the Faithworks Charter in your church, project or organisation, look up details on the website www.faithworks.info or contact the Faithworks office.

Five

A Call to Action

'Politics is too serious a matter to be left to the politicians.'

Charles De Gaulle

This chapter is divided into six sections looking at key ways of getting involved in the local political process and working to build strong, trusting, productive relationships.

1   How to get to know your local MP.
2   What is a hustings meeting and how are they run?
3   How does local government work?
4   What is a local strategic partnership?
5   How to join a political party.
6   How to stand for election as a local councillor.

'One of the penalties for refusing to participate in politics is that you end up being governed by your inferiors.'

Plato

It is not uncommon to hear people talking about politics in cynical tones. It is very easy to stand on the sidelines and criticise. However, if we want to see a positive change in the political process, it is our responsibility to do something about it. Politics belongs as much to the electorate as it does to the elected.

> '*Politics is based on the indifference of the majority.*'
> James Reston

The starting point for our involvement in the world of politics is simply to cast a vote on polling day. In an age in which more young people voted in the 'Pop Idol' competition than in the 2001 general election and only 32.8% of the electorate registered a vote in 2002's local elections, carefully considering the issues and taking the time to cast a vote has become extraordinary.

But further to that, if we are serious about implementing this radical manifesto of trust, building strong, trustworthy relationships is vital. In order to stand a chance of building such relationships with our political leaders, as with anyone else, the responsibility is ours to make the first move, to seek the opportunity to open and maintain lines of communication. And, as we have seen, because trust is a two-way street, as we work to build our involvement in our communities, others (local residents, businesses, other voluntary groups and churches, as well as politicians) will find us more trustworthy. When we withdraw, we have no influence. When we engage, we will increasingly find that our opinions are not only heard, but also sought. And as we build trusting relationships, we will also find that we win the right to talk and be heard about the issues our communities face.

1 How to Get to Know Your Local MP

One of the first steps in developing a greater involvement in, and understanding of, the political process is to get to know your local Member of Parliament. Your local MP is responsible for representing the views and concerns of their constituents to central government. Obviously, the more meaningful contact they can have with active members of their constituency, the more effectively they can fulfil their task. The busyness of their office means that, unless you initiate and maintain a relationship with your MP, it simply won't happen – so take the first step. Remember that every politician is a human being just like any other. Much of the time the correspondence they receive is negative, complaining about what they have not done or loading them with new responsibilities and unrealistic expectations. You could begin to build a good relationship with your MP simply by writing to them (either as an individual or as a church) to offer them some encouragement, support, praise or help.

Every MP faces a hugely difficult job – any decision they make or stance they take will inevitably upset or offend someone. Frequently they are charged with not listening to people's views; though, of course, what is actually meant is 'You didn't do what I told you to do!' In order to build a trusted relationship with your MP, treat them well even when they make a decision or back a policy with which you are unhappy.

You can find out who your MP is by:

- Asking in your public library or local town hall.
- Phoning the House of Commons Public Information Office (020 7219 4272).
- Visiting the 'Constituency Locata service' at: www.locata.co.uk/commons.

Once you have done this, you can contact your MP by:

Writing

The best way to contact your MP is to write to them at the House of Commons, London, SW1A 0AA. Writing a letter to introduce yourself, invite them to an event or to present any issue you have, is a good idea as it allows you to explain yourself clearly and means that they can then refer to the written details of your case, question etc. Below are five tips for writing a positive letter.

- Keep it short – no more than two A4 pages.
- Make sure it is easy to read – if possible, type it.
- If you are writing your letter by hand only use blue or black ink.
- Remember that letters packed with biblical quotes often do not get read!
- Always be polite, courteous and reasoned.

E-mail

Most MPs can be contacted using e-mail. You can check the list of MPs at the parliamentary website: www.parliament.uk/commons/lib/almsped.

Phone

You can telephone your MP's office at the House of Commons by phoning the switchboard (020 7219 3000) and asking to be put through to the appropriate extension.

Constituency surgeries

Most MPs hold advice centres when they are available in their constituency for constituents to discuss issues with them. Details are usually found in the local press, public libraries or through your MP's secretary or local party office.

Visiting Parliament

Members of the public are entitled to visit and attend debates in Parliament. Tickets for debates can be obtained through MPs. When the Commons is sitting, the public are allowed access to Central Lobby to see their MPs.

Public Information Office

Further enquiries about the work, proceedings and history of the House of Commons should be directed to the House of Commons Information Office.

> House of Commons Information Office
> House of Commons
> London
> SW1A 2TT
>
> Tel: 020 7219 4272
> Fax: 020 7219 5839
> E-mail: hcinfo@parliament.uk

For information about contacting your MP in Scotland, Wales or Northern Ireland, visit Care's Change Activist website: www.changeactivist.org.uk (Care is one of Faithworks' partner organisations. See p. 93).

2   What is a Hustings Meeting and How Are They Run?

Elections provide a natural opportunity for us to engage in the process of politics and involve others. In the weeks running up to any election, and especially a general election, the public is more alert to what politicians have to say about policy formation and are keener to interact with them.

A hustings meeting gives an opportunity for interested members of the public to listen to and question the various political candidates standing for election as MPs or councillors about their policies and attitudes. By running a hustings meeting, the churches of your town create for themselves not only the chance to question the candidates, but also a great way of serving the entire community – providing local residents with a forum in which they can express their views and engage with the candidates.

So how does one go about setting up a hustings meeting?

- Essentially all you need is a venue, an audience and the candidates. It's worth remembering, though, that in the run-up to an election, the political parties will be hugely busy running their campaigns. However, the candidates will almost certainly be keen to attend a meeting set up by a group of local churches. It is important, though, to get in early; contact the candidate's campaign offices as soon as an election has been announced (you can even explore the possibility and set tentative dates beforehand).
- It is imperative that you invite all of the candidates standing for election in your constituency to your hustings meeting (including, of course, the current post holder if they are standing for re-election). Not to do so is, in fact, against the law. It may well be that not all of the candidates will be able to attend, but it is your task to give an equal opportunity to all parties.
- You will be more likely to attract the candidates to your meeting if you can guarantee a large audience. It makes

sense, then, to work in partnership with other churches in your area and hold the meeting at the largest venue available.

- Once the hustings meeting has been arranged, the venue and date decided and the candidates invited, you should set about creating good publicity for it. Ensure that it is announced in all of the churches involved, deliver flyers to local residents, shops, offices and colleges and advertise in the local press.

- On the evening itself you will need someone competent to chair the meeting. This person will be responsible for maintaining a smooth-running debate in which all of the candidates are given equal opportunity to speak but not hog the microphone.

- In order to keep an informal atmosphere, it is a good idea to have all of the candidates and the chair of the meeting seated on the stage throughout.

- The chair should give each of the candidates a short time to introduce themselves and outline some of their policies, before opening up the debate to take questions from the audience. It's a good idea for the chair to have a list of questions in reserve in case the audience are slow to chip in.

- Ensure that the discussion doesn't become too bogged down in any one issue – the purpose of the meeting is to gain an insight into the candidates' views on a range of matters of local interest.

- A hustings meeting is a perfect setting in which to ask your local candidates how they would seek to work with churches and faith groups in an ongoing way. It is also an opportunity for you to encourage them, offer your support and make it clear to them that you are keen to work in partnership.

3 How Does Local Government Work?

Many issues that directly affect your community are the responsibility of local government. However, there is often confusion and a good deal of popular mythology about the structure and responsibility of local government. Every church should aim to build a relationship with the council or councils which govern them. Many local councils are open to the idea of working in partnership with churches and other faith groups to deliver services to the community. Of course, this will only be possible if you pro-actively go about building a relationship with, and begin to become trusted by, your local council. If nothing else, in grant applications and the like, your church will most commonly deal with government on a local level.

Your local council exists to deal with issues that are best handled at a local level. It brings democracy closer to the people and enables specific local problems to be solved directly and without outside intervention.

- Everywhere has at least one layer of local government.
- In most English counties there are two main layers – county and district councils.
- A county council will cover a population of between roughly 500,000 and 1,500,000 people.
- Each county council area contains between four and fourteen district councils, each covering a population of roughly a hundred thousand people.
- In some places county and district councils have now merged to become what are known as 'unitary' authorities. Unitary authorities include city councils and metropolitan boroughs.
- Northern Ireland, Scotland and Wales have unitary authorities across the board.

- In London, the borough councils have gained a second layer of local government, with the establishment of the Greater London Authority, and share responsibilities with it.

What are the responsibilities of a County Council?

- Education
- Social services
- Transport
- Strategic planning
- Fire services
- Consumer protection
- Refuse disposal
- Libraries
- Recreation
- Cultural matters
- Smallholdings

What are the responsibilities of a District Council?

- Local planning
- Housing
- Local highways
- Building regulation
- Environmental health
- Refuse collection
- Recreation
- Cultural matters

A unitary authority takes on all of the responsibilities of county and district councils.

Town councils and parish councils

Town and parish councils are much smaller bodies that sit below district councils in local government structure.

They represent areas with a population of up to thirty thousand people – but they are usually much smaller than that. Town and parish councils are basically the same as each other – the only difference between them is that town councils represent largely urban communities where parish councils are predominantly rural. Town and parish councils have very limited responsibilities:

- They are generally concerned with investing in improvements to the local environment and taking action in their local communities.
- They are consulted by unitary, county or district councils on planning proposals.
- They are funded by Council Tax revenue (which they are given by the higher levels of local government) and their activities tend to be limited by their financial resources.

New style local councils

Councils have traditionally set up committees to run individual services, and only major decisions like the annual budget have been made by the full council. However, reforms introduced by central government in 2000 now require councils to replace the committee system with one of the following:

- A cabinet-style administration.
- A directly elected mayor and cabinet.
- A directly elected mayor and council manager.

Most councils have opted for one of the first two models. In both, the task of the remaining councillors is to scrutinise the work of the executive.

Who are the representatives?

- County, district and unitary councils, as well as the Greater London Authority, are composed of democratically elected councillors or assembly members.
- There are more than twenty thousand councillors in the UK, at the time of writing and around 88% of them are affiliated to a political party – the remaining 12% being independent.
- Council members receive no salary but can claim allowances (GLA members and members of each council's executive, however, are salaried).
- The number of seats on councils depends on the size of the population of the area it governs.
- Councillors are normally elected by the public every four years.
- In some authorities, elections are held every year.

What do councillors do?

- Make decisions.
- Monitor the overall activities of the council.
- Get involved locally.
- Network with local organisations.
- Take up issues on behalf of members of the public – casework.
- Hold regular 'surgeries' for constituents.
- Attend formal council meetings.

County, district and unitary councils operate closely with other providers of services authorised by central government (health, housing, employment, fire and police services etc.) and frequently local councillors are appointed to local boards delivering these services. Councillors, therefore, have many opportunities for providing

leadership in important areas of policy affecting millions
of lives.

Who are my councillors?

There is at least one councillor representing your ward
(the local area where you live). The best way to find out
who your councillors are is to ring the Electoral Registra-
tion Office at your local council.

   You can visit your local council and sit in on public
meetings. Give your council a call and find out when its
next public meeting will take place. By law, members of
the public are allowed to be present for most council
business.

4   What is a Local Strategic Partnership (LSP)?

There has been a seismic shift in local democracy since the
year 2000.

   The Local Government Act 2000 imposed some big
changes on the way that local authorities work. For
churches and charities, the most important of these is the
fact that local authorities now have to work more in partnership with the voluntary, business and other sectors in
their area in order to draw up and implement what's commonly called a 'community strategy'.

   This strategy includes a vision of what the local community would like their area to look like in ten to twenty
years' time, and sets priority issues which the local
authority should tackle in partnership with other local
agencies. Since so many people have a view about what
should be in this strategy and how it should be imple-
mented, bodies commonly known as 'Local Strategic Partnerships' (LSPs) have become mandatory. LSPs are

designed to be a way of bringing together all interested parties and allowing them to have a say in the strategy and also monitoring progress of the bodies responsible for implementing the strategic plan, once it has been agreed. Many LSPs have reserved places for the representatives of faith and community groups on their main boards.

Local councils and other statutory organisations such as the health service and the police, especially in the poorest neighbourhoods, now have to develop meaningful partnerships with voluntary groups, faith communities, community groups, businesses and other parties who have an interest in the area. These groups are collectively known as 'stakeholders'.

Thematic Forums and Local Area Partnerships

Because LSPs can be quite big (they have to include business people, representatives of the voluntary sector and the public services, e.g. health, police, education etc.), some LSP boards do not necessarily keep places for people from faith communities. But many local authorities have complemented the overarching LSP by creating a 'second tier' consultative mechanism. This second tier is not obligatory and does not have to take a specified format, though most function in one of the two ways below. They provide a valuable way to be a positive influence on decisions that affect your community, even if you can't get a place on the LSP:

• **Thematic Forums**. Once the LSP has identified what are the major priorities within the area, (usually around four to six issues such as drugs, young people, homelessness, environment) the LSP may decide to set up a second tier structure of Thematic Forums. Each priority issue will have its own Forum whose membership will be drawn widely from local people (professional and voluntary) who have expertise or a particular interest in that area.

- **Local Area Partnerships (LAPs)**. LAPs operate in much the same way as an LSP. However, they focus on a much smaller area – covering, say, two or three wards within a local council.

What about faith groups?

Special reference was made to the role of faith groups in the Government's guidance on Local Strategic Partnerships, issued March 2001:

> Partnerships will not succeed unless they provide real opportunities for people to express their views, to influence decisions and to play an active part in shaping the future of their communities. Special efforts must be made to involve groups that might otherwise be hard to reach, including faith, black and minority ethnic groups.
>
> Community and voluntary organisations and local people should be in a position to play a full and equal part in multi-agency partnerships on the same basis with statutory authorities and better resourced partners.

While there is not a statutory requirement for faith groups to be involved, the government has made it clear that 'Cinderella' groups (such as the previously excluded or sidelined faith groups) should be invited to the ball.

How to get involved:

- Ask to be involved – don't wait to be asked. If there isn't room for you on the LSP, there may well be a second tier group that you could join.

- Make it easy for local councils to contact you. Join up with the other churches in your area to provide an easy point of contact. Think about setting up a Local Faithworks Network (see p. 89).

5 How to Join a Political Party

Historically, Christians have been, and are still, active across all parties. A political party is simply an association of people sharing a similar approach to government and the development of society. Joining a party increases your ability to influence that approach. When choosing a political party, remember:

- To distinguish between the philosophy of the party – the underlying view of society, human dignity and responsibilities – and the specific policies, the ways in which the party attempts to express this.
- The party's basic philosophy should accord generally with your own.
- Joining a party does not mean you agree with every specific policy.
- Individual policies are important but changeable and can be challenged if they are inconsistent with the party's overall philosophy.
- Membership entitles you to vote on some party issues, to join committees formed for specific purposes, to participate in the formation of policy and to share in the selection of candidates for election at local and national level.
- Ultimately, party membership opens the way up for you to be selected as a candidate to contest an election – with the possibility of forming government, either

through being a member of a controlling group on a council or a majority party in the House of Commons.

Christians in the Conservative, Labour and Liberal Democrat parties have joined together to form a new organisation known as Christians in Politics. CIP runs a website (www.christiansinpolitics.org.uk) that will give you further help on joining one of these three main political parties though there are, of course, other options you should consider. These might include the Christian People's Alliance, the Green Party etc.

6   How to Stand for Election as a Local Councillor

Standing for your local council is an ideal way to build relationships, create trust and make a difference in your local community. It is a chance to influence local policy. And if you feel that you're being discriminated against because of your faith, what better way to improve links between the local council and faith groups? Every political party is keen to attract good-calibre councillors with time, understanding and energy to represent them at the local level; so, they need you!

The process of becoming a councillor can be divided into phases:

- **Researching**. To serve the needs and people in your locality, and specifically those in the ward in which you wish to stand, you need to invest time in getting to know your area. Your church community with its mix of backgrounds, ages and ethnicities may actually give you a head start here. Get involved in addressing a local need or campaigning to see change. This could bring about positive change for your community as well as giving you credibility and valuable contacts for the future.

- **Forging Alliances**. Around one in ten local councillors do not stand for a party and are 'independents' of some description. However, winning elections and representing others cannot be done alone. You will either need to join an official party or gather a group of dedicated supporters around you, if you are to enjoy the practical help and range of insights into the local community needed to be a successful councillor. If you take the party route, expect to invest time into attending meetings, fundraising or campaigning and building alliances. These activities are essential preparation for the time when the party will select who will be its candidate in elections. With less than a million people in Britain actually belonging to a political party, committed new hands on deck will always be welcome!

- **Nomination**. Anyone over the age of 21 can register with the Local Returning Officer and stand to be a local councillor. Most candidates are nominated by members of their own party. However, although a party does not have to nominate them, every candidate must have a proposer, seconder and eight declared supporters. In many cases, the local party will select its candidates for elections through a ballot; therefore you may have a chance to perfect your campaigning technique by winning over your party colleagues before you are even an official candidate. You do not have to live within a ward in order to be selected or elected as its prospective councillor.

- **Campaigning**. The importance of face-to-face contact with voters cannot be over-estimated. Having built alliances with the members of local groups, parties or community organisations and having developed a network of friends on whom you can rely to help deliver leaflets, put posters up and conduct a campaign, you should be well placed to entrust yourself to the local voters and their verdict on polling day.

Six

The Faithworks Movement

The Faithworks Movement exists:

- To empower and inspire individual Christians and every local church to develop its role at the hub of its community.
- To challenge and change the public perception of the Church by engaging with both media and government.

This chapter contains details on:

1 Joining the Faithworks Movement.
2 The Faithworks Charter.
3 The Faithworks Partners.

1 Joining the Faithworks Movement

There are three ways of joining the Faithworks Movement:

- Become a member.
- Affiliate your church, project or organisation.
- Create a Faithworks Local Network or affiliate to an existing network.

Faithworks Members

If you are interested in social action issues and would like to be better informed and resourced, you should consider becoming a Faithworks member. Membership is free and will ensure you are kept in touch with the Faithworks Movement. Sign up today on-line at www.faithworks.info/join.

Faithworks Affiliates

You can officially affiliate your church, Christian community project or organisation to Faithworks. This is an opportunity to belong to a recognised nationwide network, which will aid your negotiations with statutory agencies and increase your funding potential. We ask all Faithworks Affiliates to sign the Faithworks Charter as a benchmark to which they will aspire as they engage in community action. As a Faithworks Affiliate you will receive an official certificate recognising your Faithworks Affiliation and the right to use the Faithworks registered logo.

Faithworks Affiliation costs £20 per annum and entitles you, in addition to all the benefits of personal membership, to free downloads of the growing number of practical tools produced by Faithworks to assist your church, organisation or project in developing effective work in the local community. We also offer Affiliate discounts on consultancy and training and we are constantly reviewing how best we can serve you. To affiliate to Faithworks visit www.faithworks.info.

Faithworks Local Networks

You can affiliate to Faithworks as a local network of churches, projects and organisations across a town, county or region.

We ask each Faithworks Local Network to sign the Faithworks Charter. In addition we ask you to ensure that the churches and projects who join your network individually sign the charter and affiliate with Faithworks nationally, entitling them to all the benefits of affiliation for a cost of £20 per annum. However, beyond these simple principles we recognise that each local network will be unique and established in a way that is appropriate locally.

As a Faithworks Local Network, you will be offered a discount on bulk orders of Faithworks books and resources. You will also be given the opportunity to host Faithworks regional events to inspire and resource your members and beyond.

The Faithworks Public Relations Office will also work with you to provide you with press relations support, as well as helping to create a national profile whenever appropriate. Your local network will receive a specially designed Faithworks logo, which will include the name of the town, region or area in which you operate, for use on all literature and publicity that you produce in relation to your Faithworks affiliated activity.

If you would like more details about becoming or setting up a Faithworks Local Network please contact Dave Hitchcock on 020 7450 9046 or at dave.hitchcock @faithworks.info.

2   The Faithworks Charter

THE FAITHWORKS CHARTER

*PRINCIPLES FOR CHURCHES AND LOCAL
CHRISTIAN AGENCIES COMMITTED TO
EXCELLENCE IN COMMUNITY WORK AND SERVICE
PROVISION IN THE UK*

Motivated by our Christian faith we commit ourselves to
serve others by aspiring to the following standards in all
our community work.

We will provide an inclusive service to our community by:

1   Serving and respecting all people regardless of their
    gender, marital status, race, ethnic origin, religion,
    age, sexual orientation or physical and mental
    capability.
2   Acknowledging the freedom of people of all faiths or
    none both to hold and to express their beliefs and
    convictions respectfully and freely, within the limits
    of the UK law.
3   Never imposing our Christian faith or belief on
    others.
4   Developing partnerships with other churches, vol-
    untary groups, statutory agencies and local govern-
    ment wherever appropriate in order to create an
    effective, integrated service for our clients avoiding
    unnecessary duplication of resources.
5   Providing and publicising regular consultation and
    reporting forums to client groups and the wider com-
    munity regarding the effective development and

delivery of our work and our responsiveness to their actual needs.

We will value all individuals in a way that is consistent with our distinctive Christian ethos by:

1 Creating an environment where clients, volunteers and employees are encouraged and enabled to realise their potential.
2 Assisting our clients, volunteers and employees to take responsibility for their own learning and development, both through formal and informal training opportunities and ongoing assessment.
3 Developing an organisational culture in which individuals learn from any mistakes made and where excellence and innovation are encouraged and rewarded.
4 Promoting the value of a balanced, holistic lifestyle as part of each individual's overall personal development.
5 Abiding by the requirements of employment law in the UK and implementing best employment practices and procedures designed to maintain our distinctive ethos and values.

We will develop a professional approach to management, practice and funding by:

1 Implementing a management structure which fosters and encourages participation by staff at all levels in order to facilitate the fulfilment of the project's goals and visions.
2 Setting and reviewing measurable and timed outcomes annually and regularly to evaluate and monitor our management structure and output,

recognising the need for ongoing organisational flex-ibility, development and good stewardship of resources.

3   Doing all we can to ensure that we are not over-dependent on any one source of funding.

4   Implementing best practice procedures in terms of Health and Safety and Child Protection in order to protect our staff, volunteers and clients.

5   Handling our funding in a transparent and account-able way and to give relevant people from outside our organisation/project reasonable access to our accounts.

To sign the Faithworks Charter on behalf of your church or project, write to obtain a copy from:

Faithworks
115 Southwark Bridge Road
London
SE1 0AX

or visit www.faithworks.info

3   The Faithworks Partners

The Faithworks movement is built around eleven leading Christian organisations that have committed to work together to provide expertise, tools and resources to churches as they seek to engage with their local community. The following pages give further information on their ministries.

CARE

CARE is here to serve, inform and equip you. CARE offers people, ideas, information and resources to churches and individuals who are seeking to be 'salt and light' in their communities.

CARE is a charity which runs projects across the UK, making a tangible Christian difference through networks of volunteers. CARE is active in public life and undertakes practical caring initiatives which affect the lives of thousands.

CARE is here to help you be part of the answer.

Caring

Pregnancy Crisis

- offering support, advice information on all options and ongoing practical support with 160 UK centres .

Radical Care

- providing 'forever families', foster care for young people and befriending adults with learning disabilities.

Campaigning

Active Participation

- campaigning across the UK, in Brussels and the UN on issues of human dignity in family, health, education, politics and media.

Community Involvement

- training and resourcing Christians to be more effective light and salt, including over 500 school governors and hundreds participating in grassroots politics.
- seeking to provide practical support for teachers.

Communicating

Getting The Word Out

- helping the Church to be informed, active and effective with a Christian world view and publishing specialist research to inform public debate.

The Next Generation

- shaping education policy, getting resources into thousands of schools, speaking to youth about relationships, facilitating prayer networks for 2,000 schools.

National Help Lines:

- Carelink – 08457 626 536 – linking you to the care you need via a database of three thousand specialist agencies in sixty categories.
- www.carelinkuk.org – an on-line directory of specialist caring organisations.
- CARE confidential 0800 028 2228 – providing free, confidential access to advice and counselling on pregnancy and post-abortion care.

CARE – London, Glasgow, Belfast, Cardiff, Brussels

Head office:

   53 Romney Street
   London
   SW1P 3RF

   Tel: 020 7233 0455
   Fax: 020 7233 0455
   E-mail: mail@care.org.uk
   Website: www.care.org.uk
   Registered Charity No.1066963

CARE * Christian love in action * Caring, Campaigning, Communicating.

Care For The Family

Care for the Family's heart is to strengthen family life and to help those who are hurting because of family trauma.

It is our strong belief that prevention is better than cure and that's why we put so much effort into events and seminars for those with already good relationships – we want to provide quality input so that they can survive the hard times that usually do come along. Most of our programmes are specifically geared to be available to the whole community – not only the faith groups. They are often publicised by churches who see the value of such programmes to the whole of their community contacts. Previous titles include: *The Sixty Minute Marriage, Beating Burnout, Maintaining a Healthy Marriage, A Rough Guide for Dads* and *Working to Live*.

We also have a number of specific programmes that can be delivered at a local community level by those in local churches. How To Drug Proof Your Kids is an innovative programme to inform parents about the harmful use of drugs. Our latest course, Connect2, is aimed at those in the first five years of marriage. Our Training Department can provide materials and support for those who wish to run these courses and other small groups addressing marriage and parenting issues in their local area on behalf of and for any community group with which they are networked.

2004 has seen an expansion of our work with single parents, step parents, those who have been widowed at an early age and parents who have experienced the death of a child. In all these initiatives, Care for the Family works with churches to help them bring support to their local community.

Registered Office

> PO Box 488
> Cardiff
> CF15 7YY

> Tel: 029 2081 0800
> Fax: 029 2081 4089
> E-mail: mail@cff.org.uk
> Website: www.care-for-the-family.org.uk

Caritas – Social Action

Caritas – Social Action is the voice of the Catholic Church on social justice and care in England and Wales. We are a new organisation seeking to promote Catholic social action both within the Church and in society as a whole. We work with a range of organisations and individuals who are involved in the relief of poverty, the promotion of social justice and community development, for the benefit of people of all faiths and none. We are probably the largest Catholic membership organisation and the only national Catholic agency promoting social action in England and Wales.

We seek to:

- bring together those with an interest in Catholic social action and service provision to share, promote, identify, explore, affirm and improve.
- explore all communication methods to promote social action and the principles behind it.
- provide the opportunity for faith reflection which relates to poverty, social justice and care.

- gather and disseminate information.
- monitor, analyse and influence policy in England and Wales giving a greater voice to Catholic justice and welfare organisations.
- promote the development of supportive communities.

The Catholic voluntary sector is formed of a range of welfare, care and social action organisations and activists. Caritas – Social Action is the national umbrella body for these, and is the official national social welfare agency of the Catholic Church in England and Wales. Caritas members are involved in and offer a diverse range of activities across England and Wales.

There is an estimated turnover of £90 million, 6,500 employed staff, 35,000 volunteers and over 1 million beneficiaries.

These impressive statistics are only a hint of the excellent work that is going on in the Catholic voluntary sector at all levels, from innovative grass roots community work to national projects commanding considerable budgets.

For more information, advice and support contact:

> Caritas – Social Action
> 39 Eccleston Square
> London
> SW1V 1BX
>
> Tel: 020 7901 4875
> E-mail: caritas@cbcew.org.uk
> Website: www.caritas-socialaction.org.uk

Christian Herald

As the UK's only interdenominational Christian weekly newspaper, our heartbeat is the local church. Every week, our paper is packed with news of grassroots activity that is making a difference – local churches finding needs to meet, thinking creatively about serving their local community and forging partnerships to improve life for those living around them. And we report plenty of global church inspiration and challenge, too.

Christian Herald is committed to equipping Christians in a number of ways:

- By helping readers understand the contemporary issues of the day from a biblical standpoint.
- By telling the stories of local churches who are making their presence felt, day by day, in their villages, towns and cities.
- By stretching readers' thinking – stressing that the Gospel has something to say and something to do no matter what the area of contemporary life.
- By providing the information and challenge that can help stir Christians into life wherever God has placed them: work, home, school, neighbourhood.

It's our conviction that for a resurgent Church to bring the life and love of Christ to a desperately lost world, it must begin to engage with it sacrificially, humbly and passionately.

We hope to help in that process.

Russ Bravo
Editor, *Christian Herald*
Garcia Estate
Canterbury Road
Worthing
West Sussex
BN13 1EH

Tel: 01903 821082
Fax: 01903 821081
E-mail: editor@christianherald.org.uk
Website: www.christianherald.org.uk

Christianity

Christianity is a monthly magazine with a readership of over 35,000 who are drawn to its lively mix of news, analysis, columnists, reviews and loads more. Regular contributors include; Tony Campolo, Steve Chalke, Jane Collins, Margaret Ellis, Mark Greene, Joyce Huggett, Jeff Lucas and Mike Pilavachi.

This seventy-plus page magazine is culturally relevant and biblically based. It aims to reflect its tag line: real life, real faith, in the real world. The readership is drawn from right across the denominations.

Articles identify ideas, key trends, principles, programmes and initiatives which churches in the UK can learn from and adapt to their own situation. Christianity encompasses news, culture, reviews, persecuted church news, spirituality, biblical strategies, websites to visit, devotions, insight, leadership issues, theological reflection, true-life ministry stories, plus pages of jobs.

Christianity magazine is available from all good Christian bookshops price £2.80 or through your letterbox by subscription.

Save 30% off the cover price by subscribing through direct debit – twelve issues for just £23.

Telephone: 01892 652364 or
subscribe on-line at: christianitymagazine.co.uk

Don't just take our word for it:

> 'Creative, provocative and incisive, *Christianity* magazine always nudges me to think, lifts me towards hope, and prompts me to act.'
> Jeff Lucas, Spring Harvest
> Leadership team and popular speaker/author

Christianity Magazine
CCP Ltd
PO Box 17911
London
SW1P 4YX

Tel: 020 7316 1450
Fax: 020 7316 1453
E-mail: ccp@premier.org.uk

Credit Action

Credit Action is a national money education charity established in 1994. We are committed to helping people manage their money better. Our passion is to help people stay in control, rather than let money control them and disrupt their lives through over indebtedness.

We produce a range of resources, which help everybody handle their money well. Credit Action operates at a national level through advocacy, collaboration and partnerships with various groups and companies, as well as at a local level through a network of volunteers who play a vital and very varied range of roles.

We try and help as many people as possible avoid the pain of debt. However, we recognise many contacting us will be in trouble already, so we have very close links with the major debt counselling charity the Consumer Credit Counselling Service (www.cccs.co.uk) (Registered Charity No. 1016630). They provide all their debt counselling and management services totally free. Their free Helpline number is 0800 138 1111.

Whilst Credit Action has long-standing connections with the church, we are committed to working with all groups regardless of their faith or other affiliations to help everyone manage their money well.

> Credit Action
> Howard House
> The Point
> Weaver Road
> Lincoln
> LN6 3QN
>
> Tel: 01522 699777
> E-mail: office@creditaction.org.uk
> Website: www.creditaction.org.uk
> registered Charity No. 1035783

Moorlands College

Moorlands College provides a challenging learning environment where men and women, passionate about Jesus Christ, may be nurtured and equipped to impact both church and world.

As an Evangelical, interdenominational Bible College, Moorlands aims for the highest standards in delivering courses that are biblically based, academically rigorous and culturally relevant; grounding everything in practice to facilitate effective service in today's world and creating a supportive community which promotes spiritual, personal and relational maturity.

In the past decade or so, Moorlands has recognised the crucial nature of understanding what is happening to culture and building courses that equip students to engage relevantly in community work of all types in a professional and biblically coherent fashion.

Two of our most popular courses, Community and Family Studies and Youth and Community Work, resonate significantly with the Faithworks goals. For many years Moorlands has educated and trained a large number of students, who, when they graduate, have the learning, the experience and the skills to work with churches, Christian organisations and local authorities in community development work.

Through partnership with Faithworks, Moorlands will now be in a position to share specialist course content and its expertise in training and mentoring with a much wider audience – helping local churches to mobilise their members towards effective community projects.

Moorlands College
Sopley
Christchurch
Dorset
BH23 7AT

Tel: 01425 672369
Fax: 01425 674162
E-mail: mail@moorlands.ac.uk
Website: www.moorlands.ac.uk

Oasis Trust (founding partner)

Oasis Charitable Trust is an organisation committed to demonstrating the Christian faith in action. It works in communities across the world, seeking to provide holistic solutions to the major social issues of our time.

Oasis focuses its activities on the poor and marginalised in society and seeks to equip others to engage in similar work to increase the impact of the project in which it gets involved.

Oasis was founded in 1985 by Steve Chalke and it is organised into four major areas of innovative activity:

- *Community Action* – providing housing and health care to some of society's most vulnerable members, it seeks to teach life skills and break the cycle of no home, no job.
- *Global Action* – working directly and with partners in thirteen countries around the world. Through the exchange of people, expertise and resources, Oasis seeks to enable churches and communities to empower some of the world's poorest and most marginalised people.
- *Youth Action* – investing and training tomorrow's church and community leaders. It also runs social

inclusion projects across London focusing on those at risk of being excluded from the education system.

* *Church Action* – equipping the church through personnel, training, consultancy and projects. It also develops new models of culturally appropriate expressions of church for the twenty-first century. Oasis Church Action created Faithworks to enable and inspire every local church to rediscover its role at the hub of the community.

For more information about Oasis, please contact:

> Steve Chalke
> Oasis Trust
> The Oasis Centre
> 115 Southwark Bridge Road
> London
> SE1 0AX
>
> Tel: 020 7450 9000
> Fax: 020 7450 9001
> E-mail: enquiries@oasistrust.org
> Website: www.oasistrust.org

The Shaftesbury Housing Group

The Shaftesbury Housing Group is a professional charitable Christian organisation established to meet housing and care needs. As at April 2004 the Group provides homes and/or care services to over twenty thousand people, primarily in the South of England.

Shaftesbury Housing was established by the Shaftesbury Society in 1970 and is now a separate organisation. The Group's parent association and two of its subsidiaries are registered social landlords. The Group has a financial turnover of £69 million and employs approximately 1,550 staff.

The Group has a wide range of experience in relation to housing and care. This includes major urban regeneration including commercial development and training opportunities within multi-cultural communities. Specific examples are the regeneration of a thousand homes in Hackney and the provision of a community-based housing association for management and improvement of fifteen hundred homes in Oxfordshire.

The current constituents of the Group are:

- **Shaftesbury Housing Association** – Parent Association providing family homes and sheltered housing (for rent and leasehold).
- **Ashley Homes** – residential care and supported housing division.
- **Banbury Homes Housing Association** – community-based association providing family homes, sheltered housing and supported housing.
- **Kingsmead Homes Ltd** – local housing company engaged in urban regeneration, provision of family homes, training and workshop units.
- **Shaftesbury Hallmark Limited** – student and key worker housing in London.
- **Cooper Homes & Developments Ltd** – development company.

For further information please contact:

Clive Bodley
Executive Director
Shaftesbury Housing Group
1 Mawle Court
Banbury
Oxon
OX16 5BH

Tel: 01295 272451
Fax: 01295 265995
EMail: cdb@shaftesburyhousing.org.uk
Website: www.shaftesburyhousing.org.uk

Stewardship

Stewardship is the Christian financial support services charity formed by the merger of Stewardship Services and Sovereign Giving. Stewardship exists to maximise good stewardship – of individual givers, churches and charities.

Stewardship provides a range of practical services to help organisations, from getting started as a charity through to help with the ongoing needs and responsibilities that they will face. These include:

Charity formation

Stewardship has extensive experience of registering charities and understands the Charity Commission and how to present applications to avoid undue delays. They can set you up with a charitable trust or charitable company specially designed for a church-based charity serving the community.

Payroll administration

Payroll can be a big burden. Their payroll bureau service takes care of the details, producing payslips, making payment to the employee's bank account, and dealing with tax and National Insurance.

Employment Contract Pack

Specially designed for use by a Christian charity, the pack contains a model contract of employment, with a number of variations, and helpful guidance notes.

Gift Aid administration

Outsource tax-effective giving to Stewardship and enjoy fast and frequent tax recovery and release from the pressure of meeting Inland Revenue requirements.

Accounts examination service

An independent examination of accounts is a legal requirement when income reaches £10,000 pa. Stewardship is a specialist in this field. Other services include insurance advice and agency and payroll giving. Stewardship is the host of M:Power, the Christian Stewardship event.

Contact Details:

> Stewardship
> PO Box 99
> Loughton
> Essex
> IG10 3QJ
>
> Tel: 08452 26 26 27
> Fax: 020 8502 5333
> E-mail: enquiries@stewardship.org.uk
> Website: www.stewardship.org.uk
> Registered charity no: 234714

YMCA

YMCAs are Christian charities belonging to a national and worldwide movement.

Working in over two hundred and fifty locations throughout England, the YMCA reaches out to young people, families and their communities, often working with people at their time of greatest need.

Through the integrated provision of housing, training, youth work and community health and fitness facilities, we encourage, support and challenge young people to become the best that they can be in mind, body and spirit.

We aim to underpin all our work with Christian principles and work towards a society where all young people feel a sense of:

- Value and purpose – enjoying a growing self-esteem and confidence.
- Belonging and trust – with a sense of a future.

- Growth and development – positive relationships with family, friends, and the wider community.

Importantly, every YMCA is led by local people, engaging with and meeting identified local needs. These local energies are supported by national expertise.

The YMCA, through its local presence, can offer churches and Christian agencies general advice and support based on practical experience in developing and delivering community work and service provision. YMCAs are interested in working in partnership with other organisations that share its ethos and its aims. We have also developed standards of best practice for many areas of our work, in relation to staff and volunteers, and we are willing to discuss how these may be used elsewhere.

Contact details:

> YMCA England
> 640 Forest Road
> London
> E17 3DZ
>
> Tel: 020 8520 5599
> Fax 020 8509 3190
> E-mail: enquiries@ymca.org.uk
> Website: www.ymca.org.uk

Launched in February 2001, the Faithworks Movement empowers and inspires individual Christians and local churches to develop their role at the hub of their communities.

It also aims to challenge and change the public perception of the church by engaging with the media and the government.

To fulfill these aims, Faithworks encourages churches and individual Christians to work together and in partnership with other groups to deliver effective services in the local community.

It provides up-to-date information, support and training as it seeks to build the most effective social action network in the country.

At the heart of the movement is The Faithworks Charter which sets out standards for excellence in community work and service provision in the UK.

www.faithworks.info

Faithworks
The Oasis Centre
115 Southwark Bridge Road
London
SE1 0AX

Tel. 020 7450 9071